Better Homes and Garden

Cat Craft
Collection

MURDOCH BOOKS®
Sydney • London • Vancouver • New York

Contents

Cats

Members of the cat family (Felidae) first appeared about 10 million years ago. All the continents except Australia and Antarctica had their cats: in Asia, tigers and snow leopards; in Africa, lions, leopards and cheetahs; in Europe, lions; and in the Americas, mountain lions and jaguars. As well as these large cats there were the smaller wild cats, from which domesticated cats (*Felis catus*) descended. In fact, most wild cats have the 'tabby' colourings that continue to occur on many domestic cats.

All cats, large and small, are hunters by instinct, with bodies designed for killing and eating other animals, birds and fish. Except the cheetah, all can retract their claws into their padded paws, drawing them in as they run, and bringing them out again when killing prey or climbing trees—or displaying anger. Their long sensitive whiskers alert them to any obstacles in their path. Cats are nocturnal in their habits, able to see very well in dim light.

Domesticated cats

Cats were probably first domesticated in Egypt, some time before 1500 BC. Villagers probably encouraged cats to stay close to their farms to keep their stored grain safe from rats and mice. So important were cats to the Egyptians that they actually worshipped them. The cat-headed goddess Bast was venerated at Bubastis, where archaeologists found a cemetery full of mummified cats.

In ancient Rome the cat was a symbol of liberty (cats do hate to be restrained) and Romans took them throughout the Roman Empire, including Britain. Domesticated cats were in China by AD 400 and Japan by 1000. European settlers took them to the Americas, where they were established by about 1750, and to Australasia by the early nineteenth century.

Selective breeding has produced over one hundred recognised cat breeds. Probably the world's most popular breed is the Persian, but the Siamese and the Burmese are close rivals. The more bizarre breeds include the Sphinx, a hairless variety, and the Ragdoll, an uncharacteristically docile cat.

Cats in myth and literature

The importance of cats to humans is demonstrated by their many appearances in fiction, poetry and traditional tales and sayings. People can be cool cats, copy cats, fraidy (or scaredy) cats, hellcats or tom cats. They can be 'sick as a cat' (cats do vomit a lot); something really good can be described as 'the cat's pyjamas' or 'the cat's whiskers'; 'to be a cat's paw' is to be the tool of another person; and 'cat-lap' is a non-alcoholic drink.

In several fairytales intelligent cats help their owners to become rich. Puss in Boots acquires a castle and princess for his poor, young master, whom he sets up as Marquis of Carabas. Dick Whittington (in reality a medieval Lord Mayor of London) sent his cat on a trading ship to Barbary, which was plagued by rats. The country's king bought the cat for a vast sum, so making Dick's fortune.

Nursery rhymes and nonsense verses have their quota of cats, too. One of the most popular is undoubtedly:

Pussy cat, pussy cat, where have you been?
I've been to London to look at the queen.
Pussy cat, pussy cat, what did you there?
I frightened a little mouse under her chair.

It probably referred originally to Queen Elizabeth I. In more recent fiction, there is Edward Lear's much-loved 'The Owl and the Pussycat', published in his *Book of Nonsense* (1846).

Cats are not always portrayed as useful or lovable. Spiteful remarks are said to be 'catty' and those using them can be 'cats'. Cats, too, were often associated with superstitions and witchcraft. In medieval superstition Satan often took the form of a black cat, and black cats thus came to be regarded as witches' familiars. They are still sometimes thought to be unlucky, especially if one crosses your path. Cats' adeptness at avoiding injury and their ability to land on their feet suggested unnatural associations and led to the myth that a cat has nine lives.

The perfect companion

Cats sleep a lot, especially in the cooler months (on average about 16 hours a day!), and many will live into their twenties. Independent, graceful, inquisitive and playful, they stimulate extraordinary affection and their clean habits make them perfect house partners. For the true ailurophile life without a cat is unthinkable, and cats today are the preferred companions of many people.

A cat lover's dream—a house filled with cats.

Knitted tabby cat family

This beautifully detailed trio have glass eyes to give them a whimsical expression, and are dressed in cute tabby-stripe knitted outfits that are easily removed. Make the cats' coats extra soft by boiling the knitted woollen pieces before final assembly and brushing them with a stiff brush while they are still damp, a process known as 'felting'.

Finished sizes Papa Cat 28 cm high; Mama Cat 24 cm high; Baby Cat 20 cm high

Materials

All cats

DMC tapestry wool: I skein in blanc (white)

DMC Coton Perlé: I skein in dark brown (3371)

One pair each of 4 mm, 3 mm and 2 mm knitting
  needles (or the size required to give the
  correct tension)

Polyester fibre filling

Felt or fabric for each cat's nose

Two matching buttons for each piece of cat's clothing
  (omit if making for younger children)

Tapestry needle

Stitch holder

Papa Cat

Cleckheaton Country 8 ply (50 g balls): 3 balls
  dark brown; I ball rust; I ball bone; I ball blue;
  I ball white

Five 3 cm diameter plastic joints

One pair of 12 mm glass safety eyes

Mama Cat

Cleckheaton Country 8 ply (50 g balls): 2 balls
  rust; I ball dark brown; I ball bone; I ball teal;
  I ball white

Five 2 cm diameter plastic joints

One pair of 10 mm glass safety eyes

Baby Cat

Cleckheaton Country 8 ply (50 g balls): I ball
  dark brown; I ball bone; I ball pink; I ball white

Five 2 cm diameter plastic joints

One pair of 8 mm glass safety eyes

Tension

Papa Cat: 22 sts to 10 cm over stocking st, using 4 mm
  needles and Cleckheaton Country 8 ply wool

Mama Cat: 27 sts to 10 cm over stocking st, using 3 mm
  needles and Cleckheaton Country 8 ply wool

Baby Cat: 30 sts to 10 cm over stocking st, using 2 mm
  needles and Cleckheaton Country 8 ply wool

(*Note:* Knitting abbreviations explained page 94.)

Baby Cat is just so lovable. Glass eyes, a fabric nose and embroidered whiskers give him real character.

Method

Using the appropriate yarn and needles, work the head pieces, ear pieces, gusset stripes, arm pieces, body pieces, leg pieces and tail piece (the needle size will dictate the size of the cat). When working the pieces for Baby Cat unravel one strand of yarn as you knit. Use the purl side as the right side of the work.

Head

Cast on 11 sts. Work 2 rows stocking st.

3rd row: Inc in every stitch ... 22 sts.

Work 3 rows stocking st, beg with a purl row.

7th row: (K1, inc 1 st in next st) to end ... 33 sts.

Work 3 rows stocking st, beg with a purl row.

11th row: (K2, inc 1 st in next st) to end ... 44 sts.

Work 3 rows stocking st, beg with a purl row.

15th row: (K3, inc 1 st in next st) to end ... 55 sts.

Work 11 rows stocking st, beg with a purl row.

Dec row: (K3, K2tog) to end ... 44 sts.

Purl I row.

Divide for right side

Knit Papa Cat, Baby Cat and Mama Cat in the colours suggested here, or choose your own combinations.

Next row: K18, turn.

1st dec row: P2tog, purl to end ... 17 sts.

2nd dec row: Knit to last 2 sts, K2tog ... 16 sts.

3rd dec row: P2tog, purl to end ... 15 sts.

4th dec row: (K3, K2tog) to end ... 12 sts.

Muzzle: Change to bone colour and work 3 rows stocking st, beg with a purl row.

1st dec row: K2tog, knit to last 2 sts, K2tog ... 10 sts.

2nd dec row: P2tog, purl to last 2 sts, P2tog ... 8 sts.

3rd dec row: K2tog, knit to last 2 sts, K2tog ... 6 sts.

Cast off.

Gusset: Work 4 rows stocking st.

1st dec row: K2tog, knit to last 2 sts, K2tog ... 6 sts.

Work 5 rows stocking st, beg with a purl row.

2nd dec row: K2tog, knit to last 2 sts, K2tog ... 4 sts.

Purl 1 row.

3rd dec row: K2tog, knit to last 2 sts, K2tog ... 2 sts.

Cast off.

Left side

Rejoin appropriate colour to rem 18 sts and K to end.

1st dec row: K2tog, knit to end ... 17 sts.

2nd dec row: Purl to last 2 sts, P2tog ... 16 sts.

3rd dec row: K2tog, knit to end ... 15 sts.

4th dec row: (Purl 3, P2tog) to end ... 12 sts.

Muzzle: Change to bone colour and work 4 rows stocking st, beg with a knit row.

Repeat 1st, 2nd, 3rd, 4th dec row as for right side.

Gusset stripe (make seven)

Cast on 2 sts.

Stocking st 12 rows.

Cast off.

Left ear and right ear lining (make one of each)

Cast on 3 sts.

Work 2 rows stocking st.

Inc 1 st at beg of next 4 rows, then 5 sts at beg of next row ... 12 sts.

Purl 1 row.

Dec 1 st at beg of next 6 rows, then dec 1 st at each end of next 2 rows ... 2 sts.

Cast off.

Right and left ear lining (make one of each)

Cast on 3 sts.

Work 3 rows stocking st.

Inc 1 st at beg of next 4 rows, then 5 sts at beg of next row ... 12 sts.

Knit 1 row.

Dec 1 st at beg of next 6 rows, then dec 1 st at each end of next 2 rows ... 2 sts.

Cast off.

Body (make two)

Cast on 12 sts.

1st row: Knit.

2nd row: Inc 1 st in next st, purl to end.

3rd row: Inc 1 st in next st, knit to end.

Rep 2nd and 3rd rows 4 times ... 22 sts.

Inc 1 st in middle of rows 12 to 21 inclusive ... 32 sts.

Work 10 rows stocking st.

Dec 1 st at beg of each row until 14 sts rem.

Cast off.

Arms (make two)

Cast on 8 sts.

Work 2 rows stocking st.

3rd row: Inc in every stitch ... 16 sts.

4th row: Purl.

5th row: (K1, inc next st, K4 inc next st, K1) 2 times ... 20 sts.

6th row: Purl.

7th row: Inc in next st, K7, s1K1psso, K2tog, K7, inc in last st ... 20 sts.

Rep 6th and 7th rows once more ... 20 sts.

10th row: Purl.

11th row: (K1, s1K1psso, K4, K2tog, K1) 2 times ... 16 sts.

12th row: Purl.

13th row: Inc 1 st at each end ... 18 sts.

Work 3 rows in stocking st.

Inc 1 st at each end of next row ... 20 sts.

Work 5 rows in stocking st.

Inc 1 st at each end of next row ... 22 sts.

Work 5 rows in stocking st.

Inc 1 st at each end of next row ... 24 sts.

Work 7 rows in stocking st.

1st dec row: K2 (s1K1psso, K1, K2tog) 4 times, K2 ... 16 sts.

Purl 1 row.

2nd dec row: (K2tog) to end ... 8 sts.

Break yarn leaving an end, thread through sts, draw up tightly and fasten off.

Legs (make two)

Cast on 18 sts.

Work 2 rows stocking st.

3rd row: (Inc 1 st in next 2 sts, K5, inc 1 st in next 2 sts) 2 times ... 26 sts.

4th row: Purl.

5th row: (Inc 1 st in next 2 sts, K9, inc 1 st in 2 sts) 2 times ... 34 sts.

Work 7 rows stocking st.

1st dec row: K12 (K2tog) 5 times, K12 ... 29 sts.

Purl 1 row.

2nd dec row: K7 (K3tog) 5 times, K7 ... 19 sts.

Work 3 rows stocking st.

Mama Cat wears a simple striped dress. Like the rest of the family her body pieces were 'felted' for extra softness.

1st inc row: Inc 1 st in middle ... 20 sts.
Purl 1 row.
2nd inc row: Inc 1 st at each end ... 22 sts.
Work 3 rows stocking st.
3rd inc row: Inc 1 st at each end ... 24 sts.
Work 3 rows stocking st.
4th inc row: Inc 1 st at each end ... 26 sts.
Purl 1 row.
5th inc row: Inc 1 st at each end ... 28 sts.
Purl 1 row.
Next row: (K2, s1K1psso, K1, K2tog) 4 times ... 20 sts.
Purl 1 row.
Next row: (s1K1psso, K1, K2tog) 4 times ... 12 sts.
Next row: (P2tog) to end ... 6 sts.
Break yarn leaving an end, thread through sts, draw up tightly and fasten off.

Tail

Cast on 16 sts.
Work 10 rows stocking st.
1st dec row: (K2, K2tog) 4 times ... 12 sts.
Work 19 rows stocking st.
2nd dec row: (K2, K2tog) 3 times ... 9 sts.
Work 5 rows stocking st. Change yarn for tail end.
Work 10 rows stocking st.
3rd dec row: (K1, K2tog) 3 times ... 6 sts.
Purl 1 row.
Break yarn leaving an end, thread through sts, draw up tightly and fasten off.

Felting

In a large saucepan bring 3 litres of water to the boil. Add the knitted pieces and simmer for 15 minutes. Using tongs, remove the pieces from the hot water and place them under cold running water for about 5 minutes (until the yarn cools down). Wrap the pieces in a towel and squeeze out the water. While the pieces are wet, comb or brush the purl side of the pieces (right side) for a felted effect (the steel side of a pet-grooming brush works well). Leave the pieces to dry on a flat surface.

To make up cats

1 Using a flat seam, stitch the body pieces together, leaving an opening at the back. Stitch head and nose gusset tog, and join under the head seam, leaving a 3 cm opening at the back of the head. Attach safety eyes to the head, then stuff the head with polyester filling. Join inner ear pieces to outer ear pieces, then fold and stitch the ears in place. Stitch on the head stripes as shown.
2 With a strong thread take a stitch through the cat's muzzle from the eye straight down to the chin, then back up to the second eye and down to the chin again, pulling the thread slightly, to create eye sockets. Tie off the thread securely under the chin and bury the ends.
3 For the nose, cut a small triangular shape from felt (or fabric) and glue it in position, then cover it completely with straight stitches using dark brown Coton Perlé, extending the stitching below the nose for the cat's mouth as shown in the photographs.
4 Embroider the whiskers using white tapestry wool, unravelling two strands before stitching. Work each whisker as one straight stitch.
5 Place plastic joint pieces into the head and body, pull up gathers around the joints and fasten off, then snap the joints together, thus connecting the head to the body. Fold the legs and stitch seams, leaving an opening. Fold the arms and stitch seams, leaving an opening. Join arms and legs to the body using plastic joints, then stuff the limbs and body with polyester filling and stitch the openings closed.
6 Fold the cat's tail in half lengthways and then stitch it to join. Place a little of the filling in the tail and stitch it to the body.

Papa Cat's overalls
Back
First leg: Using 4 mm needles and white yarn, cast on 16 sts.
1st row: * K1, P1; rep from* to end.
Rep last row once more.
Cont in stocking st stripes of 2 rows blue and 2 rows white, work 6 rows.**
Dec 1 st at beg of next and foll alt row ... 14 sts.

Work 1 row.

Leave sts on a stitch holder.

Second leg: Work as for first leg to **.

Dec 1 st at end of next and foll alt row ... 14 sts.

Work 1 row.

Join legs. Next row: Using white yarn, K14.

Second leg sts, then knit across right side of first leg sts from stitch holder ... 28 sts.

Keeping stripes correct, work a further 7 rows, beg with a purl row.

8th row: K13, cast off 2 sts, K13.

9th row: P13, cast on 2 sts P13 (opening for tail).

Work further 10 rows.

Shape for waist: Cont in stocking st stripes, cast off 3 sts at beg of next 2 rows ... 22 sts.

Work a further 6 rows in stocking st stripes.***

Cont in white garter st for rem, work 14 rows.

Shape back neck. Next row: K4, turn.

Cont on these 4 sts only, knit 1 row.

Next row: Cast off.

With right side facing, join yarn to rem 18 sts.

Cast off next 14 sts, knit to end ... 4 sts.

Next row: Knit.

Next row: Cast off.

Front

Work as for back to ***. (Omit tail opening.)

Cont in white garter st for rem, work 6 rows.

Shape front neck. Next row: K11, turn.

Cont on these 11 sts, dec 1 st at end of every row 7 times ... 4 sts.

Knit 1 row.

Cast off.

With right side facing, join yarn to rem 11 sts, cast off 1 st, knit to end ... 10 sts.

Cont on these 10 sts, dec 1 st at beg of every row 6 times ... 4 sts.

Knit 1 row.

Cast off.

To make up

Join side seams to waist. Join inside leg seams. Join shoulder seams, or crochet button-loops to the front shoulders. Stitch buttons to the shoulders, if desired (omit if making for younger children).

Mama Cat's dress

Back

Using white yarn and 3 mm needles, cast on 44 sts.

1st row: * K1, P1; rep from * to end.

Rep last row once more.

Cont in stocking st stripes of 2 rows teal and 2 rows white, work 14 rows stocking st.

15th row: K21, cast off 2 sts, K21.

16th row: P21, cast on 2 sts, K21 (opening for tail).

Work further 12 rows stocking st.

Next row: Knit.

Next row: (P2tog) to end ... 22 sts.

Cont in white garter st for rem, work 14 rows.

Shape back neck: Work as for back of Papa Cat's overalls.

Front

Using white yarn and 3 mm needles, cast on 44 sts.

1st row: * K1, P1, rep from * to end.

Rep last row once more.

Cont in stocking st stripes of 2 rows teal and 2 rows white, work 28 rows stocking st.

Next row: Knit.

Next row: (P2tog) to end ... 22 sts.

Cont in white garter st for rem, work 6 rows.

Shape front neck: Work as for front of Papa Cat's overalls.

To make up

Join side seams to waist. Join the shoulder seams, or crochet button-loops to the front shoulders. Stitch buttons to the shoulders if desired (omit if making for young children).

Baby Cat's overalls

Use only two strands of each colour 8 ply yarn (unravel one strand as you go). Work as for Papa Cat's overalls. Use 2 mm needles, and two strands of pink yarn in place of blue.

Papa Cat's smart overalls are buttoned at the shoulder. Stitch them instead if the cats are for very small children.

Felt and fabric landscape

A thoughtful selection of patterned fabrics and felt have been precisely cut and shaped to create this beautiful picture of a cat on a balustrade. The shapes have then been placed to suggest receding hills.

Finished size Framed 44 × 34 cm; appliqué and felt picture 35 × 25 cm
Design outline On fold-out sheet E

Materials

Small pieces of fabric for the landscape and enough to make a frame
Two packets of adhesive-backed white felt rectangles (for balcony detail)
10 × 20 cm (approx.) piece of white felt (for the cat)
One sheet medium- to heavy-gauge white cardboard
44 × 34 cm piece of thin 'see-through' white fabric (voile, muslin or similar)
Sewing thread to match landscape pieces
White thread for cat's whiskers
Polyester wadding
27 × 15 cm (approx.) piece of light fabric-bonding agent
Clear, quick-drying stainless craft adhesive
One piece of cord for hanging
45 × 35 cm piece of calico or fabric of your choice
Tracing paper and pencil
Ruler
Sticky tape
Sharp scissors, manicure scissors

Cutting out

1 Photocopy the design outline on fold-out sheet E twice and cut the shapes from the copies to use as patterns; alternatively, trace the shapes using tracing paper and a pencil. Use a ruler for greater accuracy when tracing the straight lines for the felt pieces. Cut out all the shapes, paying particular attention to the curves of the felt pieces.
2 The sky shape is cut from the top of piece no. 9, and for this shape and the landscape shapes allow an extra 1 cm on each side. For nos 2, 3, 4, 5 and 6 allow 3 mm at the top and 5 mm at the bottom of each piece. For no. 7 allow 3 mm at the top; the depth will be governed by the pattern of the floral fabric (no. 8) and its position. Note that pieces 1, 3, 5, 7 and 8 are cut as whole pieces. Turn down and tack the small allowance at the top of each piece, iron firmly and then remove the tacking.
3 Reverse the patterns for pieces nos 9 and 10, and attach them with sticky tape to the paper backing on the adhesive felt. Carefully draw around the patterns, once

again using a ruler for the straight lines. Allow an extra 1 cm at the top and sides of no. 9 and an extra 1 cm at the sides and bottom of no. 10. Remove the pattern and use sharp pointed scissors to cut through the backing paper and felt. Curved manicure scissors are excellent for the rounded shapes.
4 Reverse the pattern for the cat onto the plain felt, draw around the shape with a pencil and cut it out. This ensures there is no pencil mark that could be seen on the right side.

To assemble

1 Attach a copy of the master design to a flat surface with sticky tape, lay the white 'see-through' fabric over it with the design in the centre, and tape it down. With a pencil rule lines 1 cm wider all round than the outside dimensions of the design, that is 37 × 27 cm. Trace the positions for the landscape pieces and extend them beyond the side lines. With a ruler, trace the top of the balcony, extending the side lines.

A ruler and sharp scissors are essential if you are to achieve a professional finish in this project.

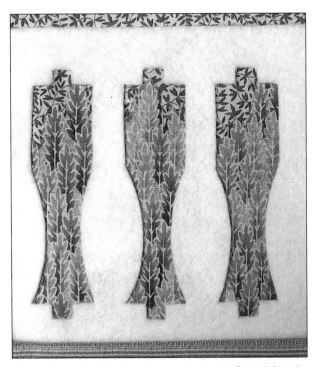

A pretty floral print fabric is used to suggest a garden glimpsed through the balcony balustrades.

2 Lift the fabric and lay it with the design centred over a piece of 37 × 27 cm wadding. Tack through the fabric and wadding close to the edges. With the exception of piece no. 7 begin applying the landscape as numbered, laying each piece over the preceding one, being guided by the pencil marks each side of the traced design, and tacking the pieces into place. Sew each landscape piece with small stab stitches through the wadding and backing fabric. Remove the tacking.

3 Bond the choice of floral fabric in the desired shape (no. 8) to no. 7, making sure the whole floral piece extends in length to 1 cm beyond the bottom line of no. 10, and stitch the fabric into place.

4 Peel away the paper on the felt cut-outs and press them into position, noting that the pieces for the post at the right-hand side meet exactly.

5 Cut a piece of wadding to fit under the cat, pin the shape into position and then stab stitch small running stitches close to the edge of the felt through all layers.

Framing

1 On the cardboard rule a rectangle 44 × 34 cm and cut it out, and then rule and cut out a frame of the same outer dimensions × 4.5 cm. On the large piece rule a rectangle 3.5 cm in from all edges, that is 37 × 27 cm. Lay the finished picture over the board, matching it to the ruled lines. Glue the excess white fabric backing to the board, keeping the edges straight and stretching the picture a little if necessary.

2 Cut strips of wadding to fit the frame and keep them in place with thin dabs of adhesive or spray adhesive. Cut the chosen fabric for the frame 8 cm wider, mitring the corners if necessary. Lay the frame wadding side down on the wrong side of the fabric, turn up 1.5 cm of fabric on the inner edges and glue into place. Press firmly with your fingers and see that the turn-up is evenly straight.

3 Apply adhesive close to the inner edges of the frame and then position the frame over the picture, matching the outer edges of the frame with the edges of the backing board. Press down firmly and allow a little time for the adhesive to set. Turn the fabric on the frame over both layers of cardboard, glue the top and bottom into place and then glue the sides.

4 Glue the required length of hanging cord into place on the back.

5 Turn under the edges of the calico and attach it to the back of the picture with small hemming stitches.

The three-dimensional shape of the picture has been cleverly enhanced by placing wadding under the white cat shape.

The picture has been given a sense of perspective and a three-dimensional quality by using felt for the foreground shapes and light fabrics for the overlapping hills.

Cards with paper cats

These charming cards feature motifs that would suit a variety of occasions, and the fact that they have been specially made by the giver is sure to bring as much pleasure as the greeting inside. Have fun choosing papers of different colours and textures, and swap the motifs around for an endless range of catty cards.

Finished size Motifs made to fit cards of 15 × 10.5 cm
Motifs On fold-out sheet A

Materials
21 × 15 cm lightweight cardboard for each base card
Paper in your choice of colour (gold paper as used in these examples is very effective)
Glue stick
Scissors
Tracing paper
Pencil
Felt-tipped pens (selection of contrasting colours)

Base cards
1 Neatly fold the lightweight cardboard to make a 15 × 10.5 cm card.
2 Trace, cut out and assemble the motifs following the instructions given below, and then glue them to the prepared cards.

Cats on a brick wall
1 From the cardboard cut a strip 11.5 × 4.5 cm and on it mark the brick design found in the pattern, using a felt pen in a contrasting colour. Glue the wall motif to the previously prepared base card as shown.
2 Cut the cats from colourful wrapping paper and glue them on top of the wall.
3 Cut flowers and leaves from coloured paper and glue them along the bottom of the wall.

Black cat
1 Cut a piece of white card 9.5 × 7.5 cm and glue it to the base card as shown.
2 Cut the cat from black paper, place a length of narrow ribbon around its neck and glue the ribbon at the back so the ends will not be seen. Glue the cat to the card.
3 From gold paper cut out a circle for the moon, and glue it to the card.

Cat in profile
1 Cut out the cat in two shades of lightweight card or paper, as indicated on the pattern. Glue the pieces to the card, noting that the legs are glued on top of the body.
2 Cut a small piece of white paper and glue it in position for an eye. Draw the pupil with a felt-tipped pen.
3 From gold paper cut out the crescent moon and the star, and glue them to the card.
4 Cut out a red paper bow, glue it to the cat's neck, and add detail with a felt-tipped pen.

Front-facing cat
1 Cut out a circle 7.5 cm in diameter and glue it to the card as shown.
2 Cut out the cat's head, legs and tail from darker paper and its body from a paler shade of paper. Glue these pieces to the card.
3 From red paper cut out a bow, glue it to the cat's neck and add detail with a felt-tipped pen.
4 Mark the eyes and nose with a felt-tipped pen.

These attractive cards are created using the most basic materials and craft skills. Even very young cat lovers can make them.

Felt-tipped pens of different colours can be used to add as much, or as little, detail as you like to the basic shapes, but you could also use carefully shaped paper pieces for features such as the cats' eyes, noses and mouths.

KEYS

Key rack with ginger cat

If you're always losing your keys or putting them down and forgetting where,
this key rack is the answer. It's simple and fun to make—and it's also a perfect perch
for a friendly carved and painted ginger cat.

Finished size 30 × 22 cm
Patterns for backboard and cat On fold-out sheet A

Materials

One piece of 100 × 180 × 9 mm thick medium density
    fibreboard (MDF)
One piece of 250 × 150 × 4 mm thick MDF
One sheet of 120 grit abrasive paper
Small bottle of craft adhesive
One pair of small mounting plates plus screws; or small
    screw eyes and cup hooks; or double-sided tape
Five square cup hooks (to hang keys)
Two 38 mm 6 gauge round head screws
One sheet of A4 carbon paper
Jo Sonja acrylic paints in gold oxide, titanium white,
    pine green, carbon black, pink
250 mL acrylic clear sealer
Fine-point permanent marker and ruler (optional)
Artist's brushes: 25 mm and 3 mm
Lettering stencil (optional)
Tools
Coping saw or jig saw
Sanding cork
Screwdriver to match
Drill with 3 mm drill bit

Cutting out

Backboard
1 Cut out the shape from the pattern on fold-out sheet
A. If you want to enlarge the design, you can use a grid
system and redraw it, or use a photocopier. Trace the
whole pattern onto the 9 mm MDF using a piece of
carbon paper placed between the pattern and the job.
2 Cut out the shape with a jig saw, or by hand with a
coping saw. Sand the edges with 120 grit abrasive paper.
3 Drill a 3 mm hole in the position for the hooks as
marked on your pattern.

Cat
1 Using the pattern on fold-out sheet A and carbon
paper, draw the cat outline onto the 4 mm MDF board.
Cut out the shape and sand the edges smooth.
2 Trace the cat's face onto a second piece of 4 mm
MDF. Cut and sand the edges as before.

Preparation for painting

Note: Paint all the parts individually before construction.
1 Undercoat all the parts with a solid coat of white
acrylic undercoat (we have used titanium white).
2 Trace the face and body details of the cat lightly in
pencil onto your cut-outs as a guide for painting.

Painting the backboard

1 To provide a light background for the cup hooks,
measure in 13 mm from each end and 13 mm down
from the top and up from the bottom. Join these four
points to form a rectangle.
2 Leaving the rectangle white, use the 25 mm brush to
paint the front of the backboard in gold oxide.
3 Outline the rectangle in black using the tip of the
3 mm brush. Alternatively, you may choose to use a fine-
point permanent marker and ruler.
4 Mark the word 'KEYS' on the backboard. In this
example we have used a lettering stencil for the outline,
and painted it with the 3 mm brush using a combination

Simple woodworking and painting skills are all you need to achieve this lovely key rack.

The cheerful cat is given the illusion of fur by lightly flicking the edges of the dark tabby stripes when the paint is almost dry.

of pine green and titanium white. The shadow effect was created using a mixture of gold oxide and black paint. However, you may choose to purchase self-adhesive letters from a craft shop or hardware store.

Painting the cat's body

1 To create the light fur stripes, mix gold oxide and titanium white paint together and apply a light coat in a tight zigzag motion, leaving the stomach and paws white.
2 To make the dark stripes, use gold oxide paint and apply it in a similar fashion.
3 When the stripes are nearly dry, use your brush to lightly flick the edges of the dark stripes into the light stripes, creating an illusion of fur.
4 Outline the legs and tail with gold oxide.

Painting the cat's face

1 Outline the ears in gold oxide. Lightly apply the mixture of gold oxide and titanium white to the face with an upward motion.

2 To create the darker fur, use the gold oxide paint and an almost dry brush, making sure that you do not overdo the effect.
3 Outline the eyes and the inside of the mouth in black. Paint the centre of the eyes dark green, leaving a white area around the green and a white spot inside the circle of green. Paint the cat's whiskers black. Outline the mouth in gold oxide and paint the tongue pink. Complete the features around the eyebrows, nose and jaw in gold oxide.

To finish the painted pieces

1 Allow the painted pieces to dry thoroughly and then rub out any pencil lines.
2 Seal all the key rack parts with two coats of clear acrylic sealer.

To assemble

1 Apply a couple of drops of craft adhesive under each piece and fix them into position.

2 Screw the mounting plates to the back of the rack. You may choose to simply use small screws and cup hooks, or even double-sided tape. Whichever method you use, you will require one on each side to help keep the rack stable on the wall when in use.

3 The keys will be hung on square cup hooks attached to the face of the rack. To determine the position of the hooks, measure up 50 mm and 30 mm in from each end of the backboard. Use a pencil and lightly mark these positions, which represent the first and last hook. Measure the distance between these points and divide it by the number of hooks you require. In this example there is a total of five cup hooks spaced approximately 60 mm apart.

4 Drill a 3 mm hole at these positions and screw your cup hooks in.

5 Hang your key rack by holding your rack in the required position, making sure it is level. Drill through the existing hole on the mounting plates into the wall. Use two 38 mm 6 gauge wood screws for fixing to the timber; if the wall is hollow, you may require specialised hollow wall anchors or star plugs for masonry.

SAFETY HINTS

Working with MDF

MDF means medium density fibreboard. It is an ideal material to work with for projects such as the painted key rack, as it does not require finishing. However, you should be aware that it does contain chemicals that can cause skin problems in some people. Always work out of the sun when using MDF. You should wear gloves if you have sensitive skin, and protect your eyes, nose, mouth and lungs from the dust.

Using power tools

All power tools are potentially dangerous. You should keep your tools in good condition, and the workplace where they will be used should be kept clean and neat, with nothing lying about that you could trip on. Power tools should ideally be connected to a power outlet via a current imbalance interrupter to protect you from electric shock in the event of an accident.

Position for hooks

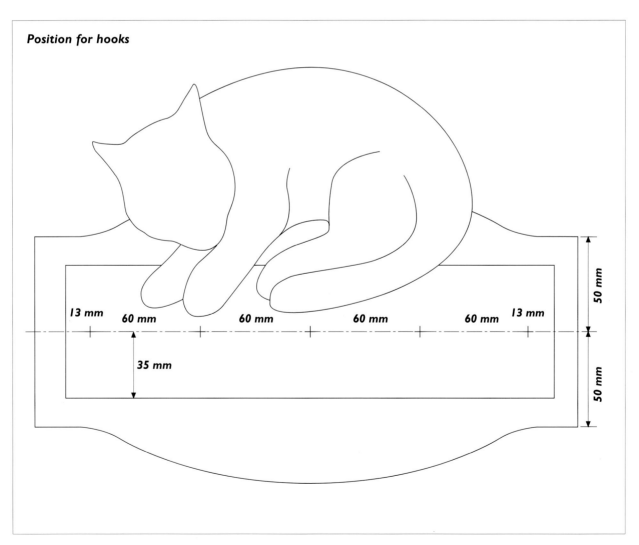

A cat's life heirloom quilt

Each of the many moods of a lively cat are illustrated in the panels, or 'blocks', of this quirky, brightly coloured quilt. In this project traditional quilting skills are applied to the creation of a distinctly contemporary design.

Finished size 160 × 120 cm
Quilt motifs On fold-out sheet B

Materials

2 m total of light-coloured fabric prints for background
1.5 m total of fabric scraps for cat motifs
0.25 m total of fabric scraps for the other shapes
    (e.g. ball, butterfly)
2 m total of dark fabric scraps (to be stitched together)
    for sashing, or a single 2 m piece of dark fabric
2 m of bonding medium
Tracing paper
Pencil

Note: When you use a bonding medium to attach shapes, you end up with a mirror image of the original. The motifs on the fold-out sheet have been reversed for you so that the image in each block of the finished quilt will face the same way as shown on the plan below.

Plan of finished quilt blocks

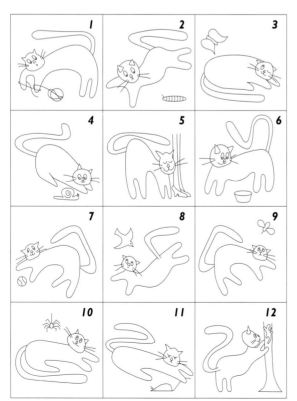

The cheeky cat shapes are fixed to the panels with bonding medium, and satin stitch is then used to sew around the cat outline.

Cutting out

For each panel:

1 From light-coloured fabric cut out a square measuring 31 × 31 cm.

2 Using tracing paper and a pencil, trace the desired cat motif from fold-out sheet B and transfer the outline onto the bonding medium. Cut out each part of the cat's body separately, as shown, and iron each piece of the bonding paper onto the wrong side of a different scrap of fabric, for a contrasting effect.

3 Cut out the fabric around the bonding medium shape, pull off the paper and then arrange the fabric pieces on the background square, to form the whole cat body. When the pieces are correctly arranged, iron them onto the background, without using steam, to bond them.

To sew

Using satin stitch, sew around the outline of each shape. In this example, satin stitch has been used for all of the details, such as the whiskers, eyes, nose and mouth. You

This wonderful quilt is just the right size to spread on a child's cot.

Step A: Use tracing paper and a pencil to trace the cat motif found on fold-out sheet B.

Step B: Trace the outline onto bonding medium and cut out each body part separately.

Step C: Iron each bonding paper shape onto the wrong side of a different scrap of fabric, then cut out the fabric around the shape.

Step D: Arrange the pieces on the fabric square to assemble the cat, then bond the pieces onto the background by ironing.

may prefer either to hand embroider them or to use a fabric pen.

Sashing

1 Cut out eight 31 × 9 cm strips. Sew the strips to the right side of blocks 1, 2, 4, 5, 7, 8, 10 and 11. Join blocks 1 and 2, 4 and 5, 7 and 8, 10 and 11. Then join blocks 2 and 3, 5 and 6, 8 and 9, 11 and 12.

2 Cut five 105 × 9 cm strips. Sew them widthwise between the above rows of blocks, as well as to the top and bottom of the quilt.

3 Cut four 160 × 9 cm strips. Sew them lengthwise between the rows of blocks and to the two sides.

To assemble

1 Cut the backing fabric and the wadding to match the quilt. Lay down the backing, with the wrong side up, and on top of this place the wadding and then the pieced quilt, with the right side up. Pin and baste all of these layers together.

2 Using small running stitches, quilt through all of the layers. You should use a variety of patterns when you quilt through the cat blocks (but note that you should not quilt over the cats or other motifs). For example, you can sew cross-hatched designs, diagonal lines, pairs of horizontal lines and swirling patterns. You should stitch parallel horizontal lines along the horizontal sashes and borders on the quilt, and use vertical lines for the vertical sashes and borders.

3 For the binding, cut out 3 cm wide strips of contrasting fabric and turn in the long edges. With the right sides of the fabric together, stitch around the edges of the quilt, turn the binding to the back and then slip stitch the binding in place.

Appliquéd and embroidered cat

Transform a plain ready-made T-shirt with this 'mixed media' design. The sheen of Paua shell button 'flowers' adds a subtle glow to the gentle shades used for the simply embroidered garden and the floral-print appliqué.

Finished size Appliqué 26 × 24 cm
Appliqué pattern On fold-out sheet A

Stitches
Chain stitch
Detached chain stitch
Ladder stitch
Stem stitch
Straight stitch

Materials
T-shirt
Four 2 cm Paua shell buttons
Three 1.5 cm Paua shell buttons
One 1 cm Paua shell button
Freezer paper (available in patchwork shops)
Water-soluble pen
Pencil
Four 20 × 15 cm pieces of small-floral patterned fabric
8 × 8 cm piece of cream cotton (for cat face shape)
8 × 8 cm piece of iron-on interfacing
DMC stranded embroidery cotton in dark mint green (3816), pale mint green (3813), medium royal blue (792), grey (648)
Hand appliqué needle size 12
Tapestry needle size 26

Button flowers and embroidered stems
1 Refer to the design on page 25 and mark the stem lines using the water-soluble pen.
2 For stems 1, 2, 4, 6 and 7 use two strands of DMC cotton in dark mint green (3816) and embroider in chain stitch. For stems 3, 5 and 8 use two strands of pale mint green (3813) and work in stem stitch. Use the tapestry needle for this embroidery.
3 When you have completed the embroidery, sew on the buttons, referring to the design when positioning the different sizes.

To prepare the appliqué
1 Wash and iron all fabrics before you begin to cut out.
2 With the pencil trace the cat body shapes on fold-out sheet A onto the rough side of the freezer paper, with no seam allowance.

3 For each piece of the cat's body, place the shiny side of the freezer-paper template on the wrong side of the appropriate piece of fabric. Use plain white cotton fabric for the face shape. Set the iron on 'wool' and press the freezer paper onto the fabric. Cut out the shapes with a 0.6 cm seam allowance.
4 Fold the seam allowance over the freezer paper and tack through both layers, turning a little at a time. Snip the fabric if necessary to make it lie flat.
5 When all shapes have been prepared, iron them, and then remove the tacking stitches and the freezer paper.

To attach the appliqué
1 Place the main shape in the centre of the T-shirt, covering the base of the embroidered stems, and tack around the edges.
2 Using a thread matching the colour of the T-shirt, with the appliqué needle ladder stitch the main shape in place, working in small stitches.
3 Place all the other shapes except for the face shape in position, and then ladder stitch them in place.

Head
1 Place a circle of white iron-on interfacing, with no seam allowance, on the back of the face shape. This will prevent the background fabric from showing through.

The cat's features are embroidered using stem stitch, while the flowers are sewn in chain stitch and stem stitch.

Embroidery placement

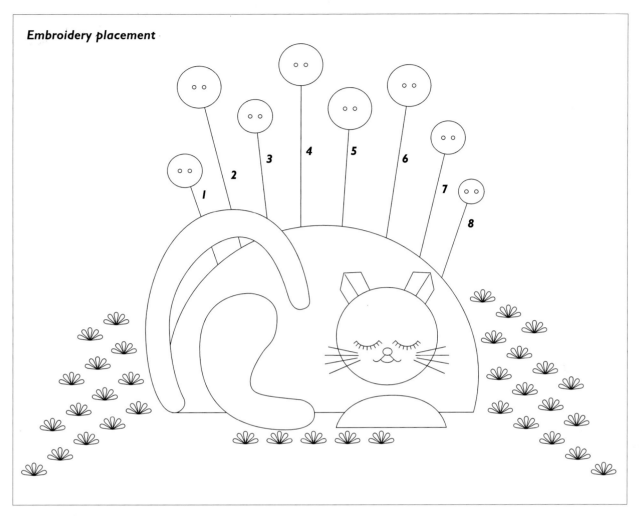

2 Mark the eyes and nose free hand and embroider them in stem stitch, using one strand of medium royal blue (792) for the eyes, and one strand of grey (648) for the nose.

3 Place the head piece on the body piece and tack around the edges, leaving a small space into which the ears will be tucked.

4 Prepare the ears following the instructions below, then ladder stitch the head in place and embroider the cat's whiskers using grey cotton (648).

Ears

1 Cut two pieces of fabric to measure 4 x 4 cm. Fold each piece lengthwise, and then fold the fabric back to the centre.

2 Fold each side in slightly, tuck the ears into position in the gaps at the sides of the head piece, and then stitch them in place.

Bow

1 Cut a piece of fabric 15 x 2.5 cm. Fold the right sides together and sew a seam down the length of the tube.

2 Turn the tube inside out, tuck in the end and ladder stitch it closed.

3 Fold the fabric tube to make a bow shape, and then attach it to the base of the appliqué cat's head using straight stitches.

To embroider the flowers

Use the tapestry needle for this embroidery as it will not split the T-shirt fibres; this will mean the garment should last much longer.

1 Copy the flower motifs from the design onto the T-shirt with the water-soluble pen. Each flower consists of five detached chain stitches.

2 Embroider the leaves (the two outside stitches and the centre one) with two strands of cotton. For the lower row on either side of the cat use the darker green cotton (3816); for the rest use the lighter green (3813).

3 To work the flowers, use one strand of the medium royal blue cotton (792) and embroider around the centre green stitch. Then embroider two small detached chain stitches on each side of it. Leave some leaves without any flowers, for interest.

Contented and cosy, this appliquéd cat sleeps easily amidst a garden of flowers.

Naive-style cat with cross stitch

This charming cat, decorated with a traditional pattern of cross-stitched posies in rustic tones, will bring a touch of country style wherever it is displayed. It is worked on Aida cloth in an oatmeal shade that gives an antique, heirloom look.

Finished size 26.5 × 13 cm
Patterns/graphs On fold-out sheet C

Stitches
Back stitch
Cross stitch

Materials
Two 20 × 30 cm pieces of 14-count Aida cloth in 'Rustico' (oatmeal fleck)
Two pieces of thin calico or other plain cream cotton for lining
Tapestry needle size 24
Polyester filling
DMC stranded embroidery cotton in the colours given in the key on fold-out sheet C, plus deepest forest green (986)
Tracing paper
Pencil

The designs on the cat's prettily patterned body are embroidered in cross stitch, and its features are worked in back stitch.

Embroidery
1 Tack vertical and horizontal centre lines on the pieces of Aida cloth. Tacking more lines ten Aida 'blocks' apart would make it easier to position the embroidered motifs; otherwise carefully count from the centre lines to begin embroidering, and from each motif to the next, referring to the graph/pattern and colour key on fold-out sheet C.
2 Use two strands of black to back stitch around the eyes and nose and to define the whiskers, and four strands to back stitch the mouth.
3 Use two strands of deepest forest green (986) to back stitch the outlines of the neck band. The cross stitches on the band are worked beyond the body outline, making it easier to match the bands when assembling the cat.
4 Outline the legs and tail in back stitch using two strands of brown (869).
5 Leave the tacking stitches in place when you have completed the embroidery.
6 Iron the wrong side of the embroidered pieces, protecting the work with a damp cloth.

To assemble
1 Pin each embroidered piece to a lining piece.
2 With tracing paper and pencil trace the pattern outline on the graphs for the front and back of the cat, adding 1 cm seam allowance and marking the central vertical and horizontal lines. Cut out the patterns. Place the pattern over the embroidered piece for the front, matching the centre lines, and then pin and cut out. Do the same with the pattern for the back of the cat.
3 Remove the tacking threads and baste the Aida cloth and lining pieces together, stitching close to the edge.
4 With the right sides together pin all round the pieces, being careful to match the front and back neck bands. With a small stitch, machine a 7 mm seam, leaving an opening at the bottom for turning through.
5 Trim the seams and clip them at intervals where shown by a 'C' on the pattern, to prevent puckering. Push the ears down into the body then turn the body inside out.
6 Firmly stuff the body with polyester filling, and then neatly close the opening at the bottom.

This embroidered cat is a beautiful and ingenious example of the traditional combination of cat and flower motifs.

Embroidery pattern

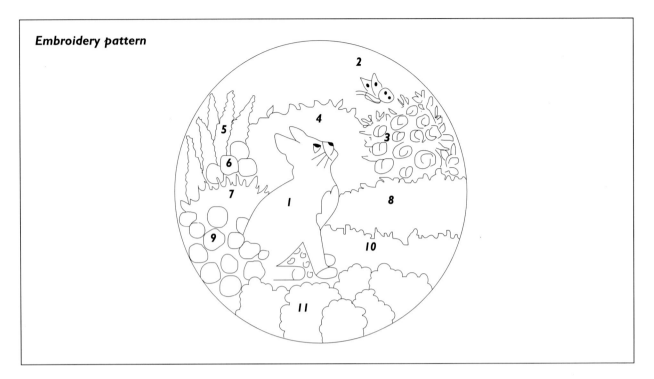

Area no. 3

Use bullion stitch with two strands of crimson (304) for the flowers and sew the leaves with two strands of leaf green (988).

Area no. 4

The flowers are scattered in three shades of pink (893, 894 and 776) and the centres in light tangerine (742), all with one strand and two twists. Work the leaves for this area of embroidery in two strands of medium dark grey-green (522).

Area no. 5

Work the flower tips with one strand of grass green (368) and one twist, grading to a few knots of two twists and continuing along the stem. Then stitch the flowers in dark coral red (349), medium rose pink (776), japonica pink (3712) and pale yellow (745) with two strands and two twists.

Area no. 6

Work the flowers in bullion stitch using one strand of white, and sew the centres in light avocado green (471) with two strands and two twists. Use two strands of very dark forest green (935) to work some short straight stitches in the background of this area.

Area no. 7

Sew the background first in straight stitches using two strands of grey-green (502). Scatter bullion stitches in two strands of medium lavender (209) and dark lavender (208).

Area no. 8

Work the background first with straight stitches in two strands of grey-green (502), and then sew a few stitches at the base of the group using one strand of dark green (500). Scatter the flowers among the green stitches with two strands and one twist of medium blue (334) and light blue (809).

Area no. 9

Sew the flowers with three strands and two twists in tangerine (741), light tangerine (742) and yellow (743), and work the centres in light brown (434) with two strands and two twists. Sew the leaves with two strands in forest green (3346), leaving space to be filled by black for the cat's body.

Area no. 10

Work the background first with straight stitches in two strands of pistachio green (320). Scatter the flowers with two strands and two twists in shades of yellow and tangerine (742, 743 and 745).

Area no. 11

Sew the flowers with three strands and two twists in white, very light coral (353), dark rose pink (891), medium rose pink (776) and orange (946). Use two strands of dark leaf green (3363) for the leaves.

To finish

Iron the embroidery on the wrong side, using a damp cloth. Your embroidered butterfly hunt is then ready to be framed and displayed.

Faithful friend doorstop

This rather well-fed cat is in fact filled with rocks and padded with polyester stuffing to make it sturdy enough to hold a door open in the strongest draughts. Its friendly face was embroidered in fine detail using padded buttonhole stitch, chain stitch and French knots.

Finished size 33 cm tall × 20 cm from tail to paws
Patterns On fold-out sheet F

Stitches

Buttonhole
Chain stitch
French knot
Herringbone stitch
Padded buttonhole stitch
Padded satin stitch
Running stitch
Stem stitch
Whipped chain stitch

Materials

115 × 50 cm piece of fabric
Fibre filling
One empty soup tin washed thoroughly and filled
   with rocks
4 × 75 cm ribbon for bow
DMC stranded embroidery cotton in rich yellow (725),
   black (310), flesh pink (224), deepest parrot green
   (890) and light yellow-green (3348)
Coton à Broder in black (for whiskers)
Strong thread (e.g. quilting thread)
Circle of heavy cardboard (or plastic ice-cream
   container lid)
Tracing paper
Pencil

Cutting out

Using tracing paper and a pencil, trace the patterns on fold-out sheet F and transfer them onto the wrong side of the fabric. Cut out the fabric, with right sides together.

Tail

1 Stitch around the tail pieces, taking a 0.5 cm seam allowance as you work.
2 Make a slash of approximately 2.5 cm in one side of the fabric and turn the tail through.
3 Stuff the tail with fibre filling and stitch the slit together as invisibly as possible. The slit should be on the side that will be placed against the cat's body.
4 Set the tail aside.

Legs

1 With the right sides of the leg pieces together, stitch along the lengthwise edges and around the foot.
2 Stuff each leg with fibre filling to approximately 12 cm. Press the remainder of the leg flat.
3 Set the legs aside until you have sewn the centre front seam of the body pieces.

Body

1 With the right sides of the body pieces together, stitch the centre front seam. Press the seam open.
2 Place the top of the legs level with the neck edge, with the legs parallel to the centre front seam. Stitch down both sides of the legs and across, just above the filling.
3 Stitch the centre back seam and clip the curve carefully. Join the side seams, leaving one side open between the asterisks shown on the pattern.
4 With the right sides together pin the base to the body and then stitch to attach. Turn the body right side out and place the cardboard circle or the lid in the base. Place the tin full of rocks inside the body and sew up the split in the side seam with small inconspicuous stitches.
5 Fill the body through the neck hole, using plenty of fibre filling so that it spreads all the way around the tin and goes right down into the base.

This durable and eye-pleasing doorstop—and that satisfied grin—will give years of pleasure to any ailurophile.

6 Fold over the raw neck edge 1 cm, and using strong thread (e.g. quilting thread) leave a 'tail' of thread and take small running stitches around the neck. Pull up these gathering threads and fasten them off. Stitch very neatly to close over the hole.

To attach the tail

1 Place the tail (with the split side against the body) into position on the back seam, and then stitch it carefully into place.

2 To make sure the tail stays fairly close to the body, sew a buttonholed bar approximately 0.5 cm from the body to the tail just forward of the side seam. (Likewise, to make sure the legs stay in position, work a small buttonholed bar from the back of the paw to the front of the body.)

To embroider facial features

Work the face on one head piece.

1 Stitch the padded buttonholed eyelet for each eye in two strands of deepest parrot green (890) and light yellow-green (3348). Chain stitch around the iris in rich yellow (725) and then outline the eye and lashes using stem stitch in black (310). Sew a rich yellow French knot in the centre of the iris.

2 Work the cat's nose in flesh pink (224) using padded satin stitch.

3 Embroider the mouth in whipped chain stitch using flesh pink.

4 Work the whiskers in straight stitches in black Coton à Broder (this can be done after the head is padded).

To assemble and attach the head

1 Make a 3 cm long slash in the back section of the head.

2 With the right sides together, stitch around the entire outline of the head.

3 Turn the fabric through to the right side and pad it with fibre filling, making sure to poke the filling well up into the ears.

4 Stitch very neatly to close the slit (herringbone stitch is suitable for this).

5 Place the head on the front of the body and stitch it firmly into position.

6 Tie the ribbon around the 'neck' and knot it to make a neat bow.

Big green eyes will look up at you with a warm greeting each time you pass through the doorway.

Catching the sun with kitty

A curled-up cat basks in the warmth of the sun's rays on this gorgeous but very easily crafted glass suncatcher, painted in appropriate tones of gold and amber. Hang this in a window and you will find you spend more time looking at your handiwork than at the view.

Finished size 20 cm in diameter
Motif On fold-out sheet A

Materials

Circular piece of glass in the size of your choice
Porcelaine 150 paint colours: amber (orange), esterel (brown), zafiro (blue) and topaz (red)
Porcelaine 150 outliner: anthracite (black)
Round brush size 4

Method

1 Have a glazier cut a circular piece of glass to your specified size, and ask for a small hole to be drilled in the top for hanging.
2 Paint the whole piece of glass in amber, working outwards from the centre using broad circular strokes. You must allow this coat to dry before giving the glass a second coat of amber.
3 Use a photocopier to make a copy of the motif on fold-out sheet A to fit the size of the glass. When the coats of amber are dry, position the glass over this pattern. Paint the darker sections of the cat's coat using esterel. Paint the sections for the ears and nose using topaz, and the eyes using zafiro. Allow the paint to dry before giving all sections a second coat.
4 Using the black outliner, complete the design by drawing in the outline of the cat's face, head and body. Extra tabby stripes can be added over the brown patches of fur for contrast.
5 Allow the painted glass to dry completely (which will take at least 24 hours) before placing the sun-catcher in a cold oven and then firing it at 150 to 160 degrees Celsius for half an hour. Turn off the oven and let the glass cool.

The painted glass can be fired in any domestic oven.

PAINTING ON GLASS

Before you purchase your paints consider the intended purpose of the item to be painted. Objects for display only, which will not be handled frequently or washed, can be painted with household gloss paints, artist's paints, or craft or household enamels. If the piece will be cleaned regularly, use special glass paints. Not all glass paints need to be fired, but for completely permanent colours it is best to use paints that are glazed by firing, easily done in a conventional oven.

You will need to work on a flat surface, and if using spirit- or acetate-based paints you should paint in a well-ventilated room. A novice should practise on a spare piece of glass before beginning the project.

Make sure the glass is dry and free of dust or grease. It is important to use the right amount of paint: too much and the colours will run, too little and the brush marks will show.

Outline comes in a tube with an applicator nozzle, and you should practise using it and controlling the flow. Always test it on some paper to check that it is flowing freely. Press firmly as you use it, and keep the nozzle free of built-up paint.

With paints and outliner, start from the edge furthest away from you and then work inwards, to avoid smudging.

This dozy cat is perfectly adapted to a round shape, but if you prefer a more irregular outline a glazier can customise the basic glass piece to your specifications.

Flying felines knitted mobile

Make these knitted acrobatic cats to hang in a child's bedroom, where their high-flying antics and bright colours are sure to bring delight. Each one is different: striped or plain coloured, sitting or standing, tail waving high or curling low.

Finished size Each cat 9 × 9 cm

Materials

Cleckheaton Country 8 ply (50 g balls): 1 ball each of
   green, blue, rust, red, yellow, white
DMC tapestry wool: 1 skein each of shade black (7624)
   and blanc (white)
One pair of 3 mm knitting needles
Polyester fibre filling
Tapestry needle
Two child-size coathangers
Paint for coathangers in a colour of your choice
Five wooden beads
Two pipe cleaners
Stitch holder
Tension
27 sts to 10 cm over stocking st, using 3 mm needles
and Cleckheaton Country 8 ply wool.
(*Note:* Knitting abbreviations explained page 94.)

Head (make one)

For all cats:
Using main colour (MC) and 3 mm needles, cast on 5 sts.
1st row: Purl.
2nd row: Inc in every stitch ... 10 sts.
3rd row: Purl.
4th row: (K1, inc 1 st in next st) to end ... 15 sts.
5th row: Purl.
6th row: (K2, inc 1 st in next st) to end ... 20 sts.
7th row: Purl.
8th row: (K3, inc 1 st in next st) to end ... 25 sts.
Work 7 rows stocking st.
16th row: (K3, K2tog) to end ... 20 sts.
17th row: Purl.
18th row: (K2, K2tog) to end ... 15 sts.
19th row: Purl.
20th row: (K1, K2tog) to end ... 10 sts.
21st row: Purl.
22nd row: (K2tog) to end ... 5 sts.
Break yarn leaving an end, thread through sts, draw up tightly and fasten off.

Ears (make two)

For all cats:
Using MC and 3 mm needles, cast on 7 sts.
Knit 4 rows garter st.
5th row: K2tog, knit to last 2 sts, K2tog ... 5 sts.
6th row: K2tog, knit to last 2 sts, K2tog ... 3 sts.
7th row: K2tog, knit to last 2 sts, K2tog ... 1 st.
Cast off.

Striped-cat body (make one)

For each two-colour striped cat:
Using MC and 3 mm needles, cast on 8 sts.
1st row: Purl.
2nd row: Inc in every st ... 16 sts.
3rd row: Purl.
Change to white, cont in stocking st stripes of 2 rows MC and 2 rows white.
4th row: K4, inc 1 st in next 2 sts, K4, inc 1 st in next 2 sts, K4 ... 20 sts.*
Work 9 rows stocking st.
14th row: K3, inc 1 st in next 4 sts, K6, inc 1 st in next 4 sts, K3 ... 28 sts.
Work 7 rows stocking st.
22nd row: (K2, K2tog) to end ... 21 sts.
Work 3 rows stocking st.
26th row: (K1, K2tog) to end ... 14 sts.
27th row: Purl.
28th row: (K2tog) to end ... 7 sts.
Break yarn leaving an end, thread through sts, draw up tightly and fasten off.**

One-colour cat body (make one)

Follow the same instructions for each one-colour (red/yellow) cat.

One-colour cat right leg

Using MC and 3 mm knitting needles, cast on 16 sts.
Work 4 rows stocking st.
5th row: K4 (K2tog) 4 times, K4 ... 12 sts.
Work 7 rows stocking st.*
Break off yarn and leave sts on a stitch holder.

These cute knitted cats would also make a wonderful set of soft toys to play with if they came down to land—on all fours of course—rather than being strung as a mobile.

One-colour cat left leg

Work as for the right leg to *.

With right side of work facing knit across the 12 sts of left leg on the knitting needle, then across the 12 sts of right leg on the stitch holder ... 24 sts.

Purl 1 row.

Next row: K8 (K2tog) 4 times, K8 ... 20 sts.

Underbody dart shaping: Cont in stocking st and dec 1 st at each end of every row until 14 sts remain.

Now inc 1 st at each end of every row until there are 20 sts.

This completes the dart shaping.

Work as for two-colour striped cat's body from* to **.

Striped-cat leg (make four)

For each two-colour striped cat:

Using MC and 3 mm needles, cast on 16 sts.

Work 4 rows stocking st.

5th row: K4 (K2tog) 4 times, K4 ... 12 sts.

Work 6 rows stocking st.

Break yarn leaving an end, thread through sts, draw up tightly and fasten off.

One-colour/blue striped cat back foot (make two)

For each one-colour cat and for blue striped cat:

Using MC and 3mm needles, cast on 10 sts.

Beginning with a P row, work 3 rows stocking st.

Next row: K4, inc 1 st in next 2 sts, K4 ... 12 sts.

Purl 1 row.

Break yarn leaving an end, thread through sts, draw up tightly and fasten off.

Tail (make one)

For all cats:

Using MC and 3 mm needles, cast on 8 sts.

Work 10 rows stocking st.

11th row: K2tog, knit to last 2 sts, K2tog ... 6 sts.

Work 11 rows stocking st.

(Change to contrast colour for blue striped cat.)

23rd row: K2, K2tog, K2 ... 5 sts.

24th row: Purl.

25th row: K2tog, K1, K2tog ... 3 sts.

Break yarn leaving an end, thread through sts, draw up tightly and fasten off.

To make up cats

Two-colour striped cats: Fold the body in half lengthwise and join the underside seam, leaving an opening. Fill the body firmly and close the opening. Fold the legs and stitch seams, leaving an opening. Fill the legs and close the opening. Attach the legs to the body as shown in the photograph below. (Omit back legs for the blue striped cat). Stitch the head seam, leaving an opening. Fill the head firmly and attach it to the body. To create an eye socket, take a stitch from the back to head front and to the back again, pulling the thread slightly. Use tapestry wool shade black (7624) to work two French knots for the eyes. For the nose work four small vertical stitches. Use white tapestry wool for the whiskers. Stitch on the ears. Fold the tail in half lengthwise and stitch to join. Place a small piece of pipe cleaner in the cat's tail and attach the tail to the body.

One-colour cat: Stitch darts together. Fold the body in half lengthwise and join the underside seam, leaving an opening. Fill firmly and close the opening. Fold the front legs and stitch seams, leaving an opening. Fill the front legs and close the opening. Attach the front legs to the body, as shown in the main photograph, by using small stitches. Fold the back feet in half lengthwise and stitch seams, leaving an opening. Fill and close the opening. Attach the smaller style back feet to the one-colour red and yellow cats and to the blue striped cat.

To assemble

Using wool (or embroidery cotton) string the cats from painted child-size coathangers that have been screwed together by the hook. Add wooden beads to the end of the lengths of wool.

Give each cute cat a set of lively features by working French knot eyes in black thread and sewing whiskers in white tapestry wool.

Making mischief papier-mâché bowl

This striking bowl in carnival colours, decorated with a mischievous cat unravelling three-dimensional balls of wool, is a stylish and sophisticated example of what can be achieved with papier-mâché. Keep the shapes simple and make the decoration as witty as you can.

Finished size 40 cm in diameter, 23 cm tall

Materials

For the papier-mâché pulp
Kitchen-tidy size bag of shredded paper
Large strong bucket
Boiling water
Blender
Mesh strainer
Large mixing bowl
Water-based hobby adhesive (adhesive in powder form)
Ground whiting (optional)
For the bowl
One large bowl for mould
One small bowl for base mould
Papier-mâché pulp (for this example two batches of pulp were used)
Petroleum jelly
Round plastic moulds for the 'wool balls' (available from craft shops)
PVA adhesive
Spoon for shaping
Fine abrasive paper
Strong adhesive
Stanley knife or hand hacksaw
Water-based sealer or acrylic undercoat
Wood filler for fine gaps (optional)
1 inch brush for base coat
Assorted smaller size brushes for design and outlining
Stencil brush (optional)
Sea sponge
Artist's acrylic paints: light blue, dark blue, red, yellow, black, white
Pencil, carbon paper, tracing paper for transferring the stencil
Cardboard
Scissors
1 inch brush for varnish
Polyurethane or water-based varnish

The 'balls of wool' are made using separate round plastic moulds.

TO MAKE PAPIER-MÂCHÉ PULP

1 Separate the shredded paper slightly so that the water can soak into all the pieces. Check that there are no pieces of shredded plastic (e.g. envelope windows) in the paper. Place the paper in the bucket and then cover it with the boiling water. Leave the paper to soak overnight in the bucket.

2 For a finer pulp, strain off the cooled water and repeat the first step. Alternatively, boil the strained-off pulp in a saucepan for 15 minutes with sufficient water to cover it.

3 Place small amounts of the paper pulp in the blender and liquidise it until the paper is broken down. It will probably be necessary to add more water to facilitate the blending process.

4 Strain the blended pulp through a strainer or squeeze it with your fingers so that the excess water is removed.

5 Place the pulp in a mixing bowl and gradually add the adhesive. If using adhesive in powder form use approximately one-half to three-quarters of a litre. For added strength you can add whiting (2 tablespoons per half litre of adhesive).

6 Use your fingers to mix the pulp and adhesive together until the mixture reaches a soft, clay-like consistency. This step must be done by hand, as mechanical mixers will not give the same result. The resulting pulp should not be too wet or it will be difficult to handle and will not dry to its proper strength. It is best to use the pulp immediately, but it should keep overnight if necessary.

TO MAKE THE BOWL
Shaping the pulp

1 Coat the inside of both bowls with a thin film of petroleum jelly, which will allow the pulp to be released when it is dry. Plastic bowls are perhaps the easiest to use for this, but glass, stainless steel and so on can also be used.

2 Take small handfuls of pulp and press them into the inside of the larger bowl. Overlap each handful slightly and smooth the pulp so you obtain an even coverage. Approximately 15 mm is a good thickness. Work around the inside of the bowl in this way and when you reach the rim smooth the top edge well.

3 Repeat the above steps using the smaller bowl that will form the base.

4 Coat the inside of the round moulds with petroleum jelly and fill them with pulp.

5 Place the bowls and moulds in the sun to dry. Then be patient, as the papier-mâché may take up to a week to dry completely.

6 After approximately two days, when the surface of the pulp is dry but the pulp is still soft underneath, burnish it with the back of a spoon dipped in adhesive. This will compact the pulp, making a smoother and stronger finished piece. The papier-mâché must be completely dry before it is painted, or moisture will seep to the surface and the paint will flake off. Before you continue check it does not either 'give' when you push on it, or bend.

To assemble

1 When the papier-mâché is dry release the shapes from the moulds. The papier-mâché will fall out quite easily, because of slight shrinkage. Lightly sand any irregularities on both bowls.

2 Cut the bottom out of the smaller bowl (which will be the base) using either a Stanley knife or a hand hacksaw, at an angle that will allow you to glue it to the larger bowl. Glue it to the large bowl with strong adhesive. Even up the base with sandpaper so that it will sit flat.

3 Glue the small 'rounds' to the outside of the large bowl with PVA adhesive. Seal the bowl and base, inside and out, with a good-quality water-based sealer or acrylic undercoat. If desired, fill any imperfections on the surface with wood filler.

Painting the bowl

1 With a brush, apply a base coat to the bowl (but not to the 'rounds') using light blue, and allow it to dry. Sponge dark blue over the light blue base coat, using the sea sponge.

2 Using the carbon paper and pencil, trace the design for the cat and transfer it to a piece of cardboard. Cut out the design. Using the cardboard as a template, place it on the frame and draw around the shape. Continue around the outside of the bowl and then repeat the cat design on the inside. Reverse the template as desired.

3 For the paw prints it is necessary to cut out the part you will paint as a stencil and then either pencil in the print or use a stencil brush to paint the paws.

4 On the inside centre of the bowl draw a circle and the curly lines to imitate strands of wool. Repeat these 'wool strands' on the outside as if they were coming from the raised 'wool balls'.

5 Paint the cats and wool first in white and then with two coats of the appropriate colour for a solid coverage. For the cats' paws you will be able to paint black straight over the blue base coat. Using a fine liner brush and black paint outline the cats and define their eyes, ears, legs and so on as shown in the design. Allow the paint to dry thoroughly.

6 Apply at least three coats of varnish in a gloss or matt finish, according to taste.

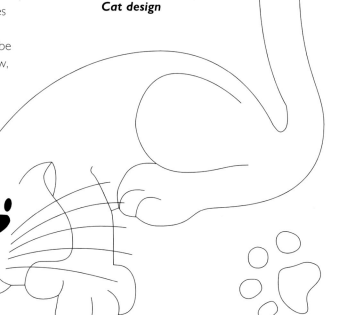

Cat design

Papier-mâché pulp may take up to a week to dry before you can paint it but the wait can be well worth it, as this stunning bowl shows.

Contented cat painted bookends

These delightful bookends would brighten any cat lover's bookshelves, but they are also extremely sturdy and practical, built from medium density fibreboard and metal using a few basic tools.

Finished size 22 x 21 cm
Cat shape On fold-out sheet C

Materials (for two bookends)
One 900 x 450 x 18 mm thick sheet of medium density fibreboard (MDF)
Four 38 mm 6 gauge countersunk wood screws
Four 40 mm panel pins
Two 200 x 50 mm pieces of light gauge sheet metal

Four 12 mm x 5 gauge countersunk wood screws
A small amount of PVA wood adhesive
One sheet of 180 grit abrasive paper
One sheet of 220 grit abrasive paper
Self-adhesive rubber bumper for base of bookends
A small amount of paint in the colour of your choice
Carbon paper
Tracing paper
Pencil

As an additional charming touch you could tie a colourful ribbon around each cat's neck before the final stage of assembly.

Tools

Panel saw or portable circular saw
Smoothing plane
Jig saw or coping saw
Flat file (smooth cut)
Half round file (smooth cut)
Pair of tin snips
Drill bits: 4 mm, 3 mm, 2 mm
Countersink bit
Electric drill
Combination square and pencil
Scotch Magic tape
Craft knife or utility knife
Stencil brush

Method

1 Using a panel saw or portable circular saw, cut one strip of MDF 120 mm wide by 900 mm long. This can then be docked off to the following lengths: two 220 × 120 mm pieces, two 190 × 120 mm pieces, and one 400 × 180 mm piece. Cut the material a little oversized. When working with a portable circular saw, use a ripping guide attached to the saw to keep the saw travelling straight; alternatively, cramp a guide to the material to achieve a clean cut.

2 Use a smoothing plane to smooth the edges back to their finished size, removing any saw marks at the same time. Make sure the edges are square.

3 With tracing paper and pencil copy the cat shape on

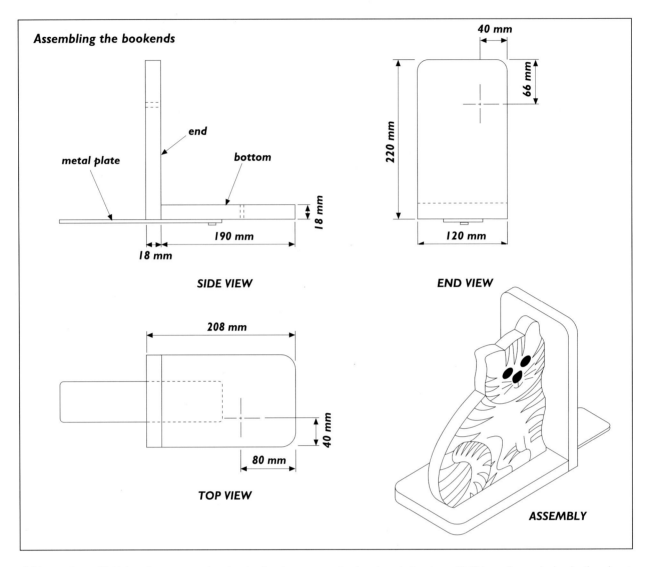

Assembling the bookends

40 mm

66 mm

220 mm

120 mm

end

metal plate

bottom

18 mm

190 mm

18 mm

SIDE VIEW

END VIEW

208 mm

40 mm

80 mm

TOP VIEW

ASSEMBLY

fold-out sheet C. Using the copy and a sheet of carbon paper trace the outer shape onto the remaining piece of MDF. Save the copy and carbon paper for later tracing.

4 Use a jig saw or coping saw to carefully cut out the cat shapes. Clean the edges up with a flat file for the outer curves and a half round file for the inner curves.

5 Assemble the angle pieces using the 40 mm panel pins and a small amount of PVA adhesive. Use the combination square to mark a line on the angle pieces 40 mm in from the front edge. Measure down from the top 66 mm and in from the end 80 mm. These are the positions of the screw holes for the screws that will hold the cats in place. Use a 4 mm drill bit to drill the clearance holes for the screws. On the outside of the angles countersink the holes with a countersink bit.

6 Hold the cats in position and drill the 3 mm pilot holes for the screws. Screw the cats into position using the 38 mm 6 gauge screws.

7 Cut two pieces of sheet metal 200 x 50 mm. These will be fixed to the bottom of the bookends, protruding so that the books sit on the pieces of metal and so hold

the bookends in place. Drill two 4 mm holes in the sheet metal 20 mm in from one end and 30 mm apart. Screw on the sheet metal so 100 mm is under the bookends and 100 mm protrudes from the bookends. Disassemble the bookends, except for the angle, ready for painting.

Painting the bookends

1 Sand all pieces well with 180 grit abrasive paper, and paint them with white undercoat. Sand the undercoat with 220 grit abrasive paper, apply the first coat of base colour and allow it to dry. Sand the parts again with 220 grit paper, then apply a second coat, and let this dry.

2 With a craft knife or utility knife, cut out the areas of the cat shape copy needed to form a stencil. Lay this over the cat. Secure the stencil with Scotch Magic tape.

3 Put the paint in a saucer or a lid. Load the stencil brush with paint, wipe as much paint as possible back into the saucer and brush any excess onto some newspaper. This prevents the paint running and bleeding under the stencil.

4 Reassemble the bookends after painting and place a self-adhesive rubber bumper on the bottom.

Embroidered hotwater bottle cover

Treat cold toes to a little softness and warmth at bedtime by making this luxurious hotwater bottle cover from cosy woollen blanketing. As a finishing touch embroider the cover with a playful kitten.

Finished size Motif 19 x 9 cm; cover 22 x 36 cm (width may vary, to fit the size of your hotwater bottle)
Pattern for cover On fold-out sheet C

Stitches

Back stitch
Chain stitch
Colonial knots
Split stitch
Stem stitch
Straight stitch

Materials

Two 40 x 40 cm pieces of white/cream wool blanketing
Two 40 x 30 cm pieces of lining fabric
15 x 5 cm of Tear-Away stabiliser fabric
Two small buttons
Appleton crewel wool in light blue (461); darker blue (743); lavender blue (891); light green (352); darker green (401); peach (706); light yellow (841); darker yellow (471); light brown (694); medium brown (695); dark brown (696)
DMC stranded embroidery cotton in dull pink (3779), dark navy blue (939)
Silk thread in white
Packet of embroidery/crewel needles sizes 3–9
Tracing paper and pencil
Water-soluble pen

Method

Work the embroidered picture onto the blanketing before you cut out the hotwater bottle pieces.

To embroider the kitten

1 With tracing paper and pencil copy the kitten motif on page 49 and transfer the shape to the Tear-Away.
2 Place the Tear-Away 10 cm from the base of the blanketing and in the centre. Tack it in place.
3 Embroider all the lines in split stitch, using crewel wool in medium brown (695).
4 Gently remove the Tear-Away. Rip off a small piece at a time, taking care not to distort the stitches.
5 Fill in the kitten motif with split stitches in three different colours, following the colour key on page 49. Make the split stitches different sizes and place them

unevenly to give the illusion of fur. The paws, chest, ear and face have not been embroidered, as the blanketing will show through and give the effect of white patches.
6 Embroider the kitten's nose with one strand of DMC stranded embroidery cotton in dull pink (3779). Use six small straight stitches to create the nose shape, and add three or four whiskers in the white silk thread, also using straight stitches. The cat's eye consists of three small straight stitches sewn in crewel wool darker blue (743). Outline the eye in one strand of DMC stranded cotton in dark navy blue (939), with another stitch sewn across the eye.

To embroider the ball of wool and flowers

1 With the water-soluble pen, draw the ball of wool and its 'tail'. Start in the centre of the ball with one strand of crewel wool in darker blue (743) and embroider a chain-stitch circle. The ball's 'tail' is a line of stem stitches.
2 Mark the flowers and stems with the water-soluble pen. Work the flowers in two strands of crewel wool in light yellow (841), darker yellow (471), lavender blue (891), peach (706) and light blue (461), using five to six colonial knots for each cluster. To create interest put light and dark shades of wool together. Embroider the

Crewel wools create the soft embroidered design of a kitten at play. The flowers are sewn using colonial knots worked in gentle colours.

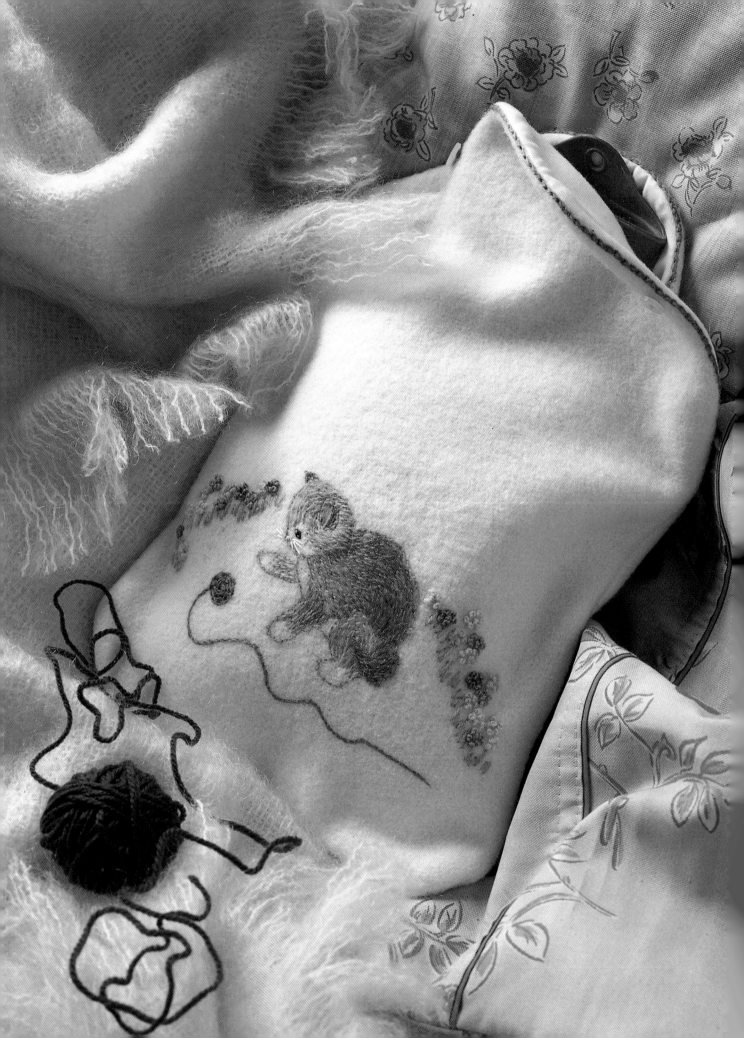

Embroidery motif

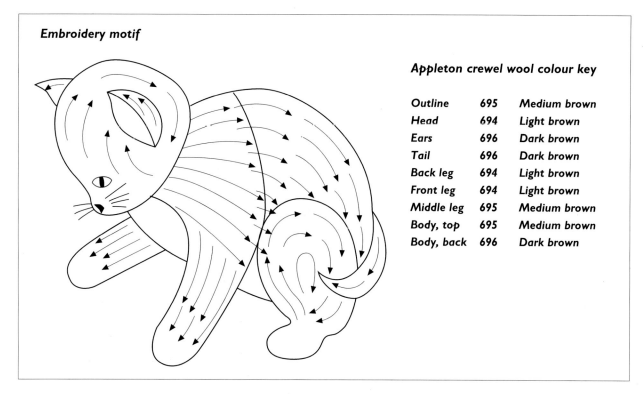

Appleton crewel wool colour key

Outline	695	Medium brown
Head	694	Light brown
Ears	696	Dark brown
Tail	696	Dark brown
Back leg	694	Light brown
Front leg	694	Light brown
Middle leg	695	Medium brown
Body, top	695	Medium brown
Body, back	696	Dark brown

stems and 'grass' in straight stitches, placing one strand of each of the green shades together.

3 After completing the embroidery, use a damp cloth to remove the marks made by the water-soluble pen.

To assemble the cover

1 Enlarge the cover pattern on fold-out sheet C to the correct size. You may need to adjust the width of the cover according to the size of your hotwater bottle. Add 2.5 cm to each side of your water bottle's diameter and then adjust the size on the supplied pattern.

2 Transfer the pattern to the wrong side of the blanketing, for both front and back pieces, and cut them out. Cut out the same pattern from the lining material.

3 Place the correct side of the front blanketing and lining together. Pin and tack the pieces across the top and sew from * to *. Repeat for the back pieces.

4 Open both pieces out and place the right sides together, blanketing on blanketing and lining on top of lining. Sew each side on the machine to create a long tube. Turn the tube outside in, so that the lining is on the outside. Make sure it is neat, then pin and tack the base together. Draw in the corners, using a plate as a guideline if need be. Sew across the base, then trim and zigzag the raw edges. Turn the cover inside out.

5 With one strand of crewel wool in darker blue (743), embroider a chain stitch in the dip between the blanketing and lining.

6 Sew on two small buttons on the front of the cover. With 50 cm of crewel wool in darker blue make a twisted cord, which will be used to fasten the buttons. Using a needle with a big enough eye to hold the twisted cord, come up through the lining on the back piece of the cover. Take a small back stitch to secure it, then cut off the knot. Loop the cord around the button to find the correct length loop and secure it with a back stitch again. Remember to knot the cord again before cutting it. Repeat for the other side.

For an attractive finish and extra strength, edge the cover in chain stitch using crewel wool.

Almost too lovely to put into the bed, this hotwater bottle cover is embroidered very simply. The white blanketing is allowed to show through to create the white patches on the kitten's face, paws and body.

Nine lives tapestry cushion

Vibrant colours against a densely stitched black background give added depth to the tapestry design on this cheerful cushion. Lighter and darker shades of a single colour are used for each of the nine cats and these colours reappear in ever-changing combinations in the panels and patterned borders.

Finished size Cushion 38 × 36 cm
Graph On fold-out sheet D

Stitch
Half cross stitch

Materials
55 × 60 cm wide 10-count Penelope canvas
Tapestry frame
70 × 115 cm fabric for back of cushion
70 cm calico for cushion insert
1.70 m of furnishing piping
35 cm zip to match back of cushion
Fibre filling
DMC Laine Colbert pure wool tapestry wool in the colours and amounts given in the key on fold-out sheet D
Tapestry needle

When embroidering this tapestry be sure to leave ample margins around the edge so it can be made into a cushion.

Cushion cover
1 Attach the canvas to the tapestry frame. Leave approximately 8 cm from the top of the canvas and make sure that there is enough room to complete the tapestry with approximately 8 cm clear at the bottom edge. Also leave a margin of approximately 5 cm at either side of the design.
2 Work the tapestry in half cross stitch according to the graph on fold-out sheet D. Use the cat design graph as a simple guide for stitching the two complementary shades of your choice. When the tapestry is complete, remove it from the frame and measure the stitched section. Allow approximately 2 cm around the edge and cut away the excess canvas.
3 Before cutting out, note that this design is not square, and all measurements must be checked. Cut a piece of fabric the same size as the worked canvas, allowing 2 cm seams, and adding 5 cm for the application of a zip, which runs crosswise near the cushion top. The cushion is longer than it is wide. Lay the fabric on the work table, measure 13 cm down from the top and cut. (There is a 2.5 cm seam allowance on each of these edges.)

4 Overlock or zigzag stitch around all the sides of both pieces. Turn under 2.5 cm on each side for the zip, and then press.
5 Affix the zip. Baste the furnishing piping around the edge so that the stitching line falls two rows into the black surround of the tapestry. Machine around using a zipper foot so that the stitching lies close to the cord without stitching into it. Pin and baste the cushion back to the cushion front. (If you open the zip approximately 10 cm before you do this it will make turning through easier.) Trim the corners. Turn through to the right side.

Cushion insert
1 Measure the finished length and width of the cushion. Cut two pieces of calico to this measurement, adding 6 cm (for seam allowance, plus extra to allow for the filling to take up).
2 Stitch around all sides of the calico, leaving an opening of approximately 10 cm for the filling. Fill the insert with fibre fill. Do not skimp on the filling, but do not overfill. Slip stitch the opening closed and place the insert into the cushion.

This cushion, reminiscent of folk-art handicraft in its use of geometric designs and bold colour, is guaranteed to make a bold statement whether displayed on a sofa or even a bed.

A CAT'S GUIDE TO ENGLAND Pat Albeck

BOXTREE

Fastidious felines cross-stitched band

Make these co-ordinating bathroom items and perform your ablutions in style.
The ready-made towel requires only the addition of a band of cross-stitched Aida cloth, while the toiletries bag is made from a matching towel. If you like you could also add a facecloth trimmed with the same embroidered cat and flowers motif.

Finished sizes Toiletries bag 26 x 22 cm, embroidered band 5 cm wide
Graph On fold-out sheet D

Stitch
Cross stitch

Materials
Towel
45 x 65 cm towel
46 x 5 cm Aida cloth band
DMC stranded embroidery cotton in the colours
   given in the key on fold-out sheet D
Matching toiletries bag
45 x 65 cm guest towel
Two 28 x 5 cm pieces of Aida cloth band
DMC stranded embroidery cotton as for
   the towel
Plastic for lining
22 cm zipper
4 cm wide bias binding to cover inside seams
Tassel to match towel colour
Tracing paper
Pencil

Towel
1 Referring to the graph and colour key on fold-out sheet D, embroider the Aida band in counted cross stitch using two threads of embroidery cotton over one square of Aida cloth. Commence the embroidery in the centre of the Aida band.
2 Turn in a narrow hem at each end of the band to fit the guest towel.
3 Machine stitch the band to the towel.

Toiletries bag
1 Embroider the Aida bands as you did for the towel, but for the toiletries bag stitch only the two centre cats and the centre three flowers.
2 From both towelling and plastic pieces cut two pieces 28 x 24 cm.

3 Tack the towelling and plastic together and treat them as one piece.
4 Insert the zipper across the top and machine stitch the Aida bands about 3 cm below the zipper (one band on each side).
5 Turn the bag inside out and machine stitch the seams, catching in the Aida bands at the sides. Cover the inside seams with bias binding.
6 Turn the bag through to the right side and attach a matching tassel to the zipper.

The cats and flowers motif has been adjusted to fit on this neat toiletries bag.

These fastidious creatures, waving their well-groomed tails, are very appropriate motifs for this towel and toiletries bag.

Stencilled gift bag and boxes

Create gift 'wrapping' that will be appreciated just as much as the present inside by applying these fun stencilled motifs to ready-made boxes or bags, and perhaps also to a matching card. The boxes and bags can continue to be used as eye-catching storage.

Finished sizes Large cat motif 10 × 8 cm; cat and mouse motif 7 × 6.5 cm; small cat motif 4 × 3 cm

Materials
Gift boxes
Gift bags
Acetate
Scalpel
Scotch Magic tape
Cardboard
Self-healing mat, or a piece of glass or cardboard
Stencil paint in black
Stencil brushes sizes 2 and 4
Spray adhesive
Tracing paper
Pencil
Kitchen paper

Method
1 With the tracing paper and the pencil, copy the stencil design, reversing it as desired.

2 Use the self-healing mat (or a piece of glass or cardboard) to protect your work table. Place the copy of the design on the mat, position it under the acetate and then tape the acetate in place to secure it. Using a new blade in the scalpel, cut out the acetate stencil with a steady hand and an even pressure.

3 Lightly spray the back of the acetate with the spray adhesive and centre it on the box or the bag, pressing down the inside edges with your finger.

4 Put some stencil paint into a saucer or plastic icecream container lid. Using a dry stencil brush, pick up a small amount of paint, then remove most of the paint from the brush on a piece of kitchen paper. With the brush, fill in the image using a circular motion or a pouncing motion. Repeat as many times as necessary to give the desired effect. One golden rule in stencilling is to use less paint than you think you need. Build up the colour using several applications, as the colour is then less likely to 'bleed' outside the image.

Stencil motifs

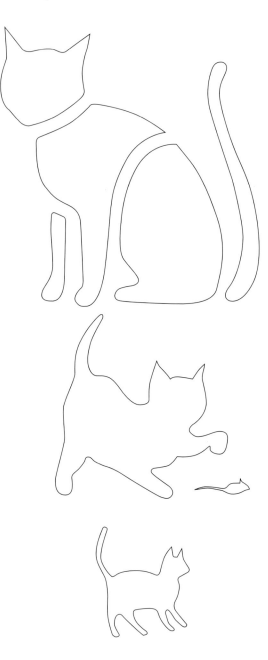

The stencilled image on these textured papers was kept sharp by using only small quantities of paint on the stencil brush. The depth of colour can be built up gradually.

Cat and mouse jumper

Delight a young child by knitting this enchanting jumper, which is as much fun to play with as it is to wear. In this novel design the cat is embroidered in tapestry wool and 'holds' its prey—a cheeky knitted mouse—in a snug pocket between its paws.

Finished sizes
Jumper To fit 3 (5) years, chest 56 (61) cm. Actual measurements: chest 66 (73) cm; approx. length 39 (43) cm; sleeve length 22 (26) cm
Mouse Finished height 10 cm
Graph On fold-out sheet C

Stitches
Back stitch
Knitting stitch embroidery
Satin stitch
Stem stitch

Materials
Cleckheaton Country 8 ply (50 g balls): 5 (6) balls blue main colour (MC); 2 (2) balls bone 1st contrast (C1); 1 (1) ball rust 2nd contrast (C2)
Patons Pure Spun 8 ply (50 g balls): 1 ball grey (for mouse)
DMC tapestry wool: 1 skein each in shades green (7911), black (7624), brown (938) and blanc (white)
One pair each 4 mm and 3.25 mm knitting needles (or the required size to give correct tension) (jumper)
One pair 3 mm knitting needles (or the required size to give correct tension) (mouse)
Tapestry needle for embroidery
Three stitch holders
Filling for mouse
Tension
22 sts to 10 cm over stocking st, using 4 mm needles and Cleckheaton Country 8 ply wool (jumper)
27 sts to 10 cm over stocking st, using 3 mm needles and Patons Pure Spun wool (mouse)
(*Note:* Knitting abbreviations explained page 94.)

JUMPER
Back
Using 3.25 mm needles and MC cast on 74 (82) sts.
1st row: K2 * P2, K2, rep from * to end.
2nd row: P2 * K2, P2 , rep from * to end.
Rep 1st and 2nd row until work measures 4 (5) cm from beg, ending with a 2nd row and inc 2 sts evenly across last row 76 (84) sts.
Change to 4 mm needles. **

The mouse can be carried around in the cat's-paw pocket, but chances are that it will spend as much time out of the pocket as in it.

The main parts of the cat's face are knitted into the front with the detail added in knitting stitch embroidery. The cat's paws, which enclose the front pocket for the mouse, are also embroidered, and they are edged in stem stitch using rust-coloured wool.

Work in stocking st (1 row K, 1 row P) until work measures 38 (42) cm from beg, ending with purl row.

Shape shoulders: Cast off 6 (7) sts at beg of next 6 rows, then 8 sts at beg of foll 2 rows.

Leave rem 24 (26) sts on a stitch holder.

Pocket lining

Using 4 mm needles and bone C1, cast on 20 sts.
Work 22 rows stocking st.
Leave sts on a stitch holder.

Front

Work as for back to **.
Work 12 (20) rows stocking st (1 row K, 1 row P).
Work rows 1 to 42 inclusive from graph.

43rd row: Place pocket, K28 (32), with right side of pocket lining facing, knit across 20 sts from stitch holder, cast off next 20 sts using bone C1 (pocket top), K28 (32).

Work rows 44 to 88 inclusive from graph.

Using MC, work 0 (2) rows stocking st.

Shape neck: Next row K32 (36), turn.

*** Dec 1 st at neck edge in alt rows until 26 (29) sts rem.

Work 5 rows. ***

Shape shoulder: Cast off 6 (7) sts at beg of next and foll alt rows 3 times in all.

Work 1 row. Cast off rem 8 sts.

With right side facing, slip next 12 sts onto stitch holder and leave. Join yarn to rem sts and knit to end.

Rep from *** to ***.

Work 1 row.

Shape shoulder: Complete as for other shoulder.

Sleeves

Using 3.25 mm needles and MC cast on 34 (38) sts.
Work 4 (5) cm in rib as for back, ending with a 2nd row and inc 8 sts evenly across last row 42 (46) sts.
Change to 4 mm needles.
Work in stocking st, inc 1 st at each end of 5th and foll

4th row until there are 56 (54) sts, then in foll 6th rows until there are 60 (64) sts. Cont without further shaping until side edge measures 22 (26) cm from beg, ending with a purl row.

Shape top: Cast off 7 (8) sts at beg of next 6 rows. Cast off rem sts.

Neckband

Using back stitch, join right shoulder seam. With right side facing and using 3.25 mm needles, knit up 78 (86) sts evenly around the neck edge, including sts from stitch holders.

1st row: K2 * P2 K2, rep from * to end.
2nd row: P2 * K2 P2, rep from * to end.
Rep 1st and 2nd row until the work measures 5 cm from beg.
Cast off loosely in rib.

To make up

1 Using tapestry wool, embroider areas in knitting stitch as indicated on the graph and colour key on fold-out sheet C. Using stem stitch embroider the outlines of the motif with Cleckheaton County rust (C2).
2 Using back stitch, join the left shoulder and neckband seam. Fold the neckband in half onto the wrong side and loosely slip stitch in position. Using back stitch, sew in the sleeves placing the centre of the sleeves to the shoulder seams. Join side and sleeve seams.

MOUSE
Body

Using Patons Pure Spun 8 ply and 3 mm needles, cast on 9 sts.
Work 2 rows stocking st (1 row K, 1 row P).
3rd row: (Inc 1st in each st) 9 times ... 18 sts.
4th row: Purl.
5th row: (K1, inc 1 st in next st) 9 times ... 27 sts.
Work 3 rows stocking st.
9th row: (K2, inc 1 st in next st) 9 times ... 36 sts.
Work 9 rows stocking st.
19th row: (K2, K2tog) 9 times ... 27 sts.
Work 9 rows stocking st.
29th row: (K1, K2tog) 9 times ... 18 sts.
Work 7 rows stocking st.
37th row: (K2tog) 9 times ... 9 sts.
Work 5 rows stocking st.
Break yarn leaving an end, thread through sts, draw up tightly and fasten off.

Ears (make two)

Using Patons Pure Spun 8 ply and 3 mm needles, cast on 16 sts.
Work 2 rows stocking st (K1, P1).

3rd row: (K2tog) 8 times ... 8 sts.
Break yarn leaving an end, thread through sts, draw up tightly and fasten off.

Tail

Using Patons Pure Spun 8 ply and 3 mm needles, cast on 4 sts.
Work 12 cm stocking st (K1, P1).
Break yarn leaving an end, thread through sts, draw up tightly and fasten off.

To make up

1 Using back stitch, join the body seam from the nose leaving an opening at the tail end. Fill firmly and then close the opening.
2 With tapestry wool black (7624) and blanc (white) embroider the eyes using satin stitch.
3 Join the side edge of each ear, then sew the ears in place. Fold the tail in half lengthways and stitch to join. Attach the tail to the body.
4 Place the mouse in the jumper pocket.

Very simple to make, this adorable knitted toy mouse goes everywhere the jumper does.

Three faces cross-stitched buttons

Display your love of cats, and add some off-beat detail to an ordinary item of clothing, by making these neat cross-stitched cat face buttons.

Finished size Motifs to fit buttons 3 cm in diameter

Stitch
Cross stitch

Materials
For each button:

29 mm self-cover button mould

6 cm square 18-count Aida cloth in white

DMC stranded embroidery cotton in the colours given in the colour key, plus black (310) and white for the whiskers

Tapestry needle size 24

Fray Stop or colourless nail polish

Embroidery
1 Following the graph and colour key for the desired motif, embroider the design in the centre of the fabric. Work in counted cross stitch, using two strands of embroidery cotton over one square of Aida cloth.

2 When you have completed the cross stitch, embroider the cat's whiskers in straight stitch, using a suitable contrasting colour.

To assemble
1 Cut out a circle 5 cm in diameter around the embroidery. Touch the edge of the circle with Fray Stop (or with a light application of colourless nail polish).

2 Gather the round edge of the circle and draw it up to cover and overlap the mould. Press in the button shank as directed on the packet.

Cross-stitch motifs

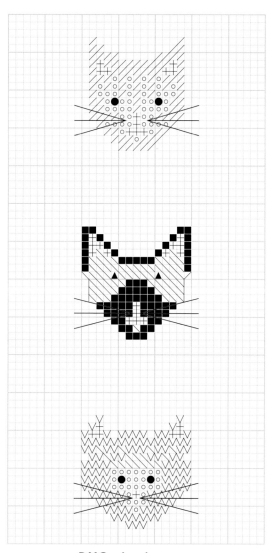

DMC colour key

/	414	*Dark grey*
+	761	*Light salmon*
●	702	*Medium bright green*
○		*White*
■	801	*Dark brown*
\	739	*Beige*
▲	995	*Peacock blue*
V	922	*Dark orange*

These charming cat faces are embroidered in counted cross stitch on Aida cloth, then fitted over a self-cover button mould.

Small projects like this one are not only fun to make, they are perfect for building up your cross-stitch confidence.

Cats and berries mockwork tablecloth

The charming 'cut-away' design on this tablecloth is actually mockwork, and the effect is achieved by clever use of simple chain-stitch embroidery and a textile marker. Even if your embroidery skills are limited you can use this technique to turn a plain cloth into a covering that is almost too pretty to cover up with an afternoon-tea setting.

Finished size Completed cat design 31 cm in diameter
Quarter design pattern On fold-out sheet A

Stitch
Chain stitch

Materials
Tablecloth
Permanent fabric marker in black
Two skeins of DMC stranded embroidery cotton
   in white
Crewel needle size 9
Pencil
Transfer pencil
Tracing paper

The motif is coloured in using a black fabric marker and then outlined in chain stitch.

To transfer the design

1 Trace the quarter design on fold-out sheet A onto tracing paper using the transfer pencil. On the wrong side of the tracing paper, trace the design again to obtain the correct image (the design would otherwise be reversed). This 'transfer' can be used again and again, but each time it is applied it will require a little longer ironing time to transfer properly.

2 Before you iron the design onto the tablecloth, make a trial design and iron that onto a scrap of fabric. This will indicate the temperature and length of time it takes for the lines to transfer. Set the temperature on the correct setting for the fabric, then place the design on the scrap piece of fabric and iron to the count of 20 to see how well it transfers. If it is not satisfactory, leave it for another few counts.

3 Centre the design on the tablecloth. Iron the quarter section, then reposition it and iron it again, pressing for a slightly longer time. Keep repositioning the design until you have completed the circle.

To colour in the design

1 When you have transferred the design, colour in the cats and the berries with the black fabric marker.

2 Set the colour by ironing both sides of the fabric. This

will enable you to wash the tablecloth and remove the transfer lines after you have completed the embroidery, without also washing out the coloured-in design.

Embroidery

1 Work all the embroidery in chain stitch using four strands of cotton in the needle. Cut a fairly long length of cotton, then separate the threads before placing them together again. This will help the chain stitch to lie flat and keep it from becoming twisted.

2 When embroidering a chain stitch note the following:
(a) When you reach the top of a point, secure it with a small back stitch before continuing. In this way the stitch will lie in a point, rather than bending around the top.
(b) When the design requires you to stitch a line running off from an existing embroidered line, come up in the previously completed chain stitch and then continue.
(c) To complete a circle, stop one stitch length in front, and take the thread around the base of this stitch and then back to complete the chain-stitch circle. In this manner you achieve a continuous chain-stitch line.

3 Embroider around the cats and berries design to give an illusion of a cut-away effect.

4 When the embroidery is completed, wash the tablecloth. Make sure that all the transfer lines have disappeared. Iron the mockwork tablecloth while it is still slightly damp.

This elegant tablecloth is so easy to create you will have plenty of time and energy left for making a matching set of mockwork napkins.

Mosaic number for a 'catty' house

A home-made house number is an expression of the style and personality of those who live within, including any feline family members, and this mosaic one is as smart as they come.

Finished size 30 x 25 cm

Materials
300 x 250.5 x 17 mm piece of plywood
Glass mosaic tiles and old china/crockery
Tile nippers
Eye protection
Tile adhesive
Grout
Rubber gloves
Palette knife
Sponge
Dry cloth
Exterior waterproofing agent

Preparation
1 Cut the plywood to size and waterproof it so that it can hang outdoors.
2 Pencil the design of your choice onto the board or copy the design from the photo opposite.
3 Wearing eye protection, cut the mosaic tiles with the tile nippers to fit your design, and break up any pieces of china or crockery that need to be in smaller sized pieces.

To fix the tiles
1 As you work, spread adhesive over only a small section of the design at a time.
2 Once all tiles and mosaic pieces are in place allow 24 hours for the adhesive to dry before you start work on the grouting.
3 Wearing rubber gloves, mix the grout according to the directions given on the packet.
4 Apply the grout with the palette knife over the entire area, ensuring that all the spaces between the tiles have been filled.
5 Using a damp sponge, remove any excess grout.

To finish
1 Let the grouted mosaic dry for 24 hours.
2 Using a dry cloth, polish the tiles to remove any powdery grouting cement film.
3 Allow the mosaic to dry for a further 24 hours before hanging the house number in position.

CUTTING AND SHAPING MOSAICS

When cutting glass mosaic tiles indoors, you will be exposed to small glass particles or glass 'dust'. It is important to shield your eyes with protective goggles. You can avoid inhaling the dust by placing the tiles on your work surface so they are to one side of, and not directly beneath, your face.

When using tile nippers hold the handles close to the end so that the force of cutting is borne by the tool's spring, not by your fingers and wrist. Place the tile so that it is just between the cutting edges of the tile nippers, with the side to be displayed facing upwards. The nippers' cutting edges should be resting on the invisible line to be cut.

To cut circles or petal shapes, the best technique is to cut off the four corners of the tile (you can draw the desired shape on the tile as a guide if you wish), and then make very small, gentle, cuts with the nippers from the outer edge of the tile, working inwards, until you have made the shape you require to fit your mosaic pattern.

Collect glass tiles and odd pieces of broken china, then let your imagination run free as you design and craft your mosaic house number.

Here is a house number that does more than just give your location—it also tells people 'a cat lover lives here'!

Buttons and bows appliquéd miniquilt

Use the basic techniques of quilting, appliqué and embroidery to create a fabric picture in subtle earthy hues that would be right at home in a country cottage.

Finished size 33 × 33 cm
Motifs On fold-out sheet C

Materials

40 cm light-coloured fabric for background
20 cm check fabric for cats
40 cm darker fabric for border
20 cm dark fabric for outside binding
Batting and calico for backing, slightly larger than quilt
Small piece of contrasting material for Suffolk puffs
Embroidery cotton: dark shade to outline cat appliqués
Four buttons
Narrow ribbon for cats' bows
Lightweight double-sided fabric bonding agent
Tracing paper and pencil
Dowel rod
Two beads
Cord

Cat appliqués

1 Using tracing paper and a pencil copy each cat motif on fold-out sheet C twice. Transfer the motifs onto the wrong side of the checked fabric and cut them out.
2 From the light-coloured fabric cut out four 12 cm background squares.
3 Iron the check cats to the background squares using the double-sided bonding agent. Buttonhole stitch around the cats with two strands of dark embroidery cotton. Embroider each cat's eyes, nose and whiskers.

To assemble the quilt

1 Join the appliquéd squares, allowing 1 cm for seams.
2 Cut four strips of the darker border fabric to a size of 22 × 7 cm. Cut four pieces of background fabric for the corners, 1 cm square, as shown. Sew two border strips to the top and bottom of the joined appliquéd squares. Sew the corner squares to each end of the remaining two border strips, allowing 1 cm seams. Stitch these strips to the sides of the joined appliquéd squares, taking care to line up the seams accurately.
3 Cut pieces of batting and calico about 4 cm larger than the quilt and tack them into position. Hand quilt the backing materials onto the joined appliquéd squares

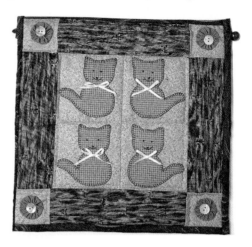

Choose brighter, contrasting colours for a more striking effect.

6 mm from the seams and down the centre seams. Trim the backing to 1 cm all around the quilt.
4 Cut four strips of binding fabric, each 8 cm wide and long enough to go around the quilt and be turned in at the corners. Fold the binding strips in half lengthwise and iron. Attach the binding strips to the two front sides of the quilt, matching the raw edges of the binding strips and the quilt. Fold the binding to the back of the quilt and hand stitch it in place. Sew the other two binding strips to the top and bottom of the quilt. Turn them under 6 mm at each end and stitch closed.
5 Cut a strip of calico 5 cm by the width of the quilt and neaten the ends. Hand stitch the calico strip to the top of the quilt backing, leaving the ends of the strip open so that the dowel rod can be inserted.

Suffolk puffs

1 Cut four circles of contrasting material 7 cm in diameter. Turn in the edges all around each circle and gather them, as shown in the photograph.
2 Stitch the puffs to the background squares at the quilt corners, and sew a button in the centre of each puff.

To finish

1 Attach a ribbon bow to each cat.
2 Insert the rod through the opening in the backing at the top of the quilt, and attach a bead at each end.
3 Stitch the ends of the cord to each side of the quilt top. Loop the cord around the rod ends several times.

Featuring a variety of different textures and decorative details, this miniquilt is a distinctively different wall-hanging.

Glamour puss cross-stitched glasses case

Make a sophisticated statement by embroidering your glasses case with this haughty Siamese, worked in sleek and stylish grey and silver tones. The gold thread of the collar gives the merest suggestion of extravagance.

Finished size Motif 12 × 6 cm
Graph On fold-out sheet C

Stitches
Back stitch
Cross stitch

Materials
Small piece of 32-count Belfast linen in pale blue-grey (small pieces may sometimes be bought from craft shops)
Satin for lining and binding
Medium weight polyester wadding
Tapestry needle size 26
DMC stranded embroidery cotton in the colours given in the colour key on fold-out sheet C
Gold thread

Embroidery
1 Cut a piece of linen 36 × 11 cm, and zigzag the edges by machine or overcast by hand. Fold the fabric in half and mark a point 14 cm up from the fold, in the centre. Commence embroidering the cat design from the ears down from this point.
2 Following the graph and colour key on fold-out sheet C, embroider the cat design in cross stitch worked across two vertical and horizontal linen threads, using two strands of embroidery thread.
3 Use one strand of black (310) to back stitch around the darkest areas (the head, feet, legs and tail) and one strand of medium dark grey (414) for the rest of the outline and the haunch. Use two strands of black cotton for the cat's mouth and the straight line across the eye, and one strand of lightest grey (762) for the whiskers and for the eyebrow.

Glasses case
1 When you have completed the embroidery, cut the satin lining the same width as the linen but 2.5 cm longer.

Next cut the padding, making it fractionally shorter than the linen.
2 Lay the padding on the wrong side of the linen, stretching it slightly along the length. Place the lining and linen with the right sides together and stitch a 7 mm seam across the three layers at both ends. Turn the lining to the back making a bound edge, and then machine stitch through all of the layers as closely as possible to the binding.
3 Pin the layers together along both sides and machine stitch them close to the edge. Fold the stitched piece in half, matching the satin bindings at the top. Baste the sides together close to the edge.
4 Cut bias strips from the satin 4 cm wide, making them longer than the case. Machine the strips to the right sides of the front 7 mm in from the edge, leaving the strips 1 cm above the starting point and 1 cm longer at the end. Turn the strips to the back and turn down the excess at each end. Fold the binding over, trimming the width if required, and hand hem.

This glasses case is padded with polyester wadding to protect the breakable contents.

Grey satin binding adds elegance and a perfect finish to this hand-made glasses case, but it is the haughty cat that makes the case so distinctive.

Motley moggies draught excluder

These six fibre-filled felines perched atop an extra-bulky draught excluder are individually made from fabric of co-ordinating patterns and colours. None of this raffish group is a pedigreed show-cat, but each has a personality and charm all its own.

Finished size 90 × 28 cm

Patterns On fold-out sheet E

Stitches
Eyelet stitch
French knot
Herringbone stitch
Padded satin stitch

Stem stitch
Straight stitch
Whipped chain stitch

Materials
Approximately 40 cm of fabric for each cat
30 × 115 cm of fabric to cover draught excluders
30 cm of calico

Each cat was given its own personality, with distinguishing features sewn on in a variety of embroidery colours and stitches, as well as appliqué details.

Two draught excluders joined with cotton tape
Stiff fishing line and black thread for whiskers
Machine thread to match fabrics
Fibre filling
Ribbons for bows
Tracing paper and pencil
DMC stranded embroidery cotton:
For eyes
Cat no. 1, grey-green (502), rich yellow (725),
    black (310)
Cat no. 2, medium eucalyptus green (3364), black (310)
Cat no. 3, brown-green (844), medium wedgewood
    blue (932), light yellow-green (3348), black (310)
Cat no. 4, dark green (500), light

tangerine (742), black (310)
Cat no. 5, light yellow-green (3348), burnt butter (782),
    black (310)
Cat no. 6, grey-green (502), light pine green (772),
    honey brown (3045), ecru
For nose and mouth
Cat no. 1, flesh pink (224)
Cat no. 2, dark dusty pink (223)
Cat no. 3, dull rose pink (3326), tongue deepest
    bright pink (309)
Cat no. 4, nose dull rose pink (3326), mouth deepest
    bright pink (309)
Cat no. 5, flesh pink (224), dark dusty pink (223)
Cat no. 6, dark dusty pink (223)

Note: You can vary the colour combinations as well as the stitches and number of threads. You can also vary the whiskers.

Cat no. 1

1 With the tracing paper and a pencil copy the pattern pieces on fold-out sheet E, adding a 0.5 cm seam allowance. Trace the pattern pieces onto the wrong side of the appropriate fabric and cut out the shapes.
2 Embroider the face on one of the head sections.
3 With the right sides of the fabric together, stitch the head sections around the edges. Make a 2 cm slash on the back of the head and stuff it with fibre filling. Stitch the slash together with small, neat herringbone stitches.
4 Make two legs in the same way, and a tail. Make the toes by taking two straight stitches where indicated on the pattern.
5 Stitch the body pieces together, leaving the neck open, and stuff the body with fibre filling. Stitch it closed with small herringbone stitches. Position the head, legs and tail on the body and stitch to attach them. Set the cat aside.

Cat no. 2

1 Choose fabric in contrasting prints and trace off the pattern pieces on the fold-out sheet. Cut out each of the fabric shapes.
2 Machine stitch 0.5 cm from the inside curve of part 1 and carefully clip the seam to the stitches. Join part 1 to part 2 along the seam line. Apply part 3 by appliqué to part 1.
3 With the right sides together, join the body sections along all sides. Make a 3.5 cm slash in the front of the body, underneath the position of the head. With the right sides together, stitch all around the tail. Slash the tail, on the back section only, and turn the tail through to the right side.
4 Fill the tail and body sections through the slashed holes and neatly close the opening using herringbone stitch. Position the tail on the front of the body and stitch it into place.
5 Work the face embroidery on one of the head sections. With the right sides together, stitch around the edge of the head and turn it through the slashed hole. Neatly close the opening using herringbone stitch, position the head on the body and stitch to attach it securely. Set the cat aside.

Cat no. 3

1 Trace off the pattern pieces and then cut out each of the fabric shapes.
2 Embroider the face.
3 Using an appliqué method apply the paws to the front lower edge of the body.

4 Stitch around the outer edge of the body and the head with the right sides together, and slash where indicated. Stuff both with fibre filling and close the slashed edges with small herringbone stitches. Position the head on the front of the body and stitch to attach it neatly and securely. Set the cat aside.

Cat no. 4

1 Trace off the pattern pieces and then cut out each of fabric shapes.
2 Embroider the face.
3 Stitch the paw lines in close zigzag.
4 With the right sides together, stitch around the body. Make a 3 cm slash in the lower back only. Turn the body through to the right side and stuff it with fibre filling. Neatly close the slit with small herringbone stitches. Set the cat aside.

Cat no. 5

1 Trace off the pattern pieces and then cut out each of the fabric shapes.
2 Embroider the face.
3 With the right sides of the fabric together, stitch around the tail. Cut a small slit in the back of the tail, turn it right side out and stuff the tail with fibre filling. Stitch around the body in the same way and fill, closing the slit with small herringbone stitches. Place the tail behind the cat and stitch it into position on the left side of the body. Set the cat aside.

Cat no. 6

1 Trace off the pattern pieces carefully and then cut out each of the fabric shapes.
2 Cut one entire body piece for the back of the cat. Trace off each of the six panels onto pattern paper, adding a 0.5 cm seam allowance on all edges. Cut out the fabric, one piece for each of the six body panels, according to whether the panel is to be a plain or a print.
3 Cut two head sections. Leave the back piece plain and appliqué the triangle piece between the ears as shown on the pattern sheet. (In the same way, appliqué the stripes onto the paws.) Embroider the face, and with the right sides of the fabric together stitch all around the outside edges of the head. Make a 3 cm slash on the back section of the cat's head, as shown on the pattern. Turn the head right side out, stuff it with fibre filling and neatly close the opening with small herringbone stitches.
4 For the body, stitch each panel 0.5 cm from the inward curve and carefully clip the edges. Join panels 1, 2 and 3 together with a 0.5 cm seam and set aside. Join panels 4, 5 and 6 in the same way. Appliqué the paws into position. Using the same method join these two sections to complete the front of the body. With the right sides

Two standard draught excluders were joined to make a perch for the feline line-up.

together, stitch around the entire body section. Make a 5 cm slash in the lower back as shown on the pattern and turn the body right side out. Stuff with filling and close the opening with small herringbone stitches.

5 For the tail, with the right sides of the fabric together stitch around the entire edge of the tail section. Make a small slash on the back of the tail section, turn the tail right side out, fill it with fibre and close the opening using small herringbone stitches. Position the tail and head on the body and stitch them in place. Set the cat aside.

To assemble the draught excluder

1 Measure the length of the draught excluders, which should be joined along their length with cotton tape. Cover the joined draught excluders with the calico fabric.
2 Cut out the covering fabric, ensuring that there is enough fabric at each end to turn under a small amount and allow the edges to come together in the centre when hand gathered.

Joining and covering the draught excluders

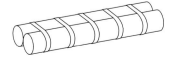 

3 Turn under 1.5 cm on the long edge of the covering material and attach it with herringbone stitch along the calico-covered door stopper. Pull the fabric securely and pin it, then stitch it invisibly and firmly. Turn under the short ends and draw up the threads to close the ends as shown in the diagram below.

Finishing the ends of assembled draught excluder

To attach the cats

Position and pin the cats along the prepared draught excluder, overlapping where necessary. With strong thread (quilter's thread, crochet thread etc.) stitch the cats into place firmly. Tie ribbon bows on the cats' necks where required.

Catch me if you can painted china

Enliven a plain set of crockery with this amusing contemporary-style border pattern. The animal chase is painted over a sponged background that highlights the stylised figures.

Materials

Inexpensive white crockery set
Porcelaine 150 paint colours: citrin (yellow), amber (orange) and lapis lazuli (blue)
Masking tape
Round brush size 3
Sea sponge

Method

1 Using masking tape, mask off the areas of the crockery not to be painted, leaving a band of china of the desired width exposed. Cover teapot and cup handles carefully.
2 Dip the sea sponge into the amber paint and lightly sponge on the colour. Allow this to dry and then sponge on a layer of the citrin colour, over the amber coat. When this is dry, remove the masking tape.
3 Once the coloured bands are dry, use the lapis lazuli paint to apply the dog, cat and mouse border pattern to the crockery freehand, trying to space the animal motifs an even distance apart. You could also make a stencil for each animal, to be applied separately. In this example the pattern has been repeated three times around the plate, and twice around the cup and teapot. Once the first application is dry, apply a second coat of lapis lazuli.
4 Allow the crockery to dry completely (which will take at least 24 hours) before placing the painted pieces in a cold oven and firing them at 150 to 160 degrees Celsius for half an hour. Turn off the oven and let the painted crockery cool.

Stencil motifs

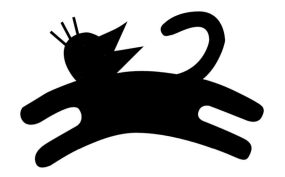

A cat's life is rarely dull—as this china shows.

With a steady hand and some china paints you can create a tea set that will inspire plenty of comment.

Tartan toms appliquéd cushion

A range of tartan fabrics are cleverly combined with plains and prints to create this very desirable cushion, and the warm colours positively invite you to snuggle close. Make one cushion and you'll be inspired to adapt the design for others, and for a matching throw.

Finished size 40 × 40 cm
Appliqué motifs, cushion pattern On fold-out sheet F

Stitches
Ladder stitch
Straight stitch

Materials
70 cm piece of check/tartan fabric for the cushion
   and the bias strips
20 cm each of six different fabrics
50 × 50 cm piece of plain background fabric
40 × 40 cm cushion insert
Three buttons
Fourteen small blue seed beads
DMC stranded embroidery cotton honey brown (3045)
Matching sewing threads
Hand appliqué needle size 12
Freezer paper (available from patchwork shops)
Satay stick (to make bias strips)
Water-soluble pen
Pencil
Ruler

Cutting out
1 Wash and iron all fabrics before starting to cut out.
2 Cut the plain background fabric for the front piece to a size of 42 × 42 cm.
3 From the main check (or tartan) fabric, first cut out the cushion pieces. Cut one back piece of 42 × 38 cm and another back piece of 42 × 21 cm, taking great care to line up the check pattern before cutting.
4 From the rest of the check fabric, cut the bias corners and bias strips (see diagram on page 78). Fold the fabric on the bias to create the four triangular corners for the cushion. Cut them out. The four bias strips for the grid pattern will be made from each of these triangles.

Bias corners and bias strips
1 Take one triangle and on the bias fold a hem of 1 cm. Do not cut it at this stage. It is easier to sew the bias

Appliquéd cats and bias bars combine to create this simple but effective design.

seam, and then cut. This bias is not designed to be turned inside out.
2 Set the needle on the sewing machine at a width that will give you a 0.5 cm seam when the sewing machine foot is at the edge of the folded fabric. Sew down the length of the bias, and then cut as close to the seam as you can.
3 Insert the satay stick (or a 5 mm bias bar if you have one) into the tube, then twist the raw edges to the back. Iron the bias strip as you pull the satay stick out of the tube. Make three more bias strips, one from each of the check triangles.
4 Make eight 12 cm long bias strips for the cats' tails using the appropriate fabrics.

Cushion front
1 Take the plain piece of 42 × 42 cm background fabric. With the water-soluble pen, mark the centre of each side, 1 cm in from the edge. Draw a line from point to point. Divide each side into three equal parts and draw lines to create a grid.
2 Pin and tack the prepared bias strips on the grid pattern and ladder stitch them in place.
3 Fold a 1 cm hem on the bias of the four triangular pieces and place them in position on the corners, taking great care to line up the check pattern properly. Pin and

Calm, sleepy, aloof and cheeky—each aspect of cat personality is shown on these simple appliqué figures.

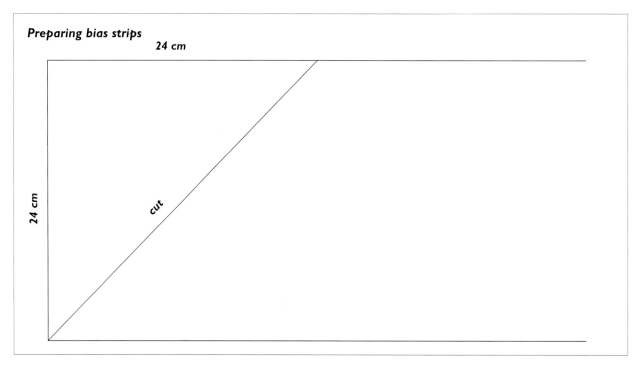

Preparing bias strips

24 cm

24 cm

cut

tack them in place and then attach them to the cushion front with ladder stitch.

4 When all the bias strips and corners are attached, remove the pen marks with a damp cloth.

Appliqué cats

1 With a pencil, trace the cat shapes on fold-out sheet F onto the rough side of the freezer paper, taking no seam allowance.

2 For each cat shape, place the shiny side of the freezer-paper template onto the wrong side of the appropriate fabric. With the iron on the 'wool' setting, press the freezer-paper template onto the fabric. Next, cut out each of the cat shapes from the fabric, taking a 0.6 cm seam allowance.

3 Fold the seam allowance over the freezer paper and tack through all the layers, turning a little at the time. Snip the fabric if necessary to make it lie flat.

4 After you have prepared all eight shapes, iron each shape and remove the tacking and the freezer paper. Place the shapes on the cushion and tack them in place.

5 Place the prepared bias strip tails on the cat shapes, then ladder stitch the cats in place using matching thread and the appliqué needle.

6 The cats' features are embroidered with one strand of stranded embroidery cotton in honey brown (3045), using straight stitches. Use the same cotton to attach the seed-bead eyes.

To assemble

1 On the two back pieces of the cushion fold a 6 cm hem. Do not sew across it.

2 Place the smaller top piece down with the wrong side up. Place the correct side of the larger bottom piece on top, with hems overlapping. Tack or pin the sides together. Trim so the pieces measure 42 × 42 cm.

3 Place the appliquéd front piece on top of the back pieces with the correct sides together. Pin or tack around all four sides. Make sure all the elements line up correctly before you stitch around the cushion. Trim the corners and zigzag the raw edges. Turn the cushion right side out.

4 The buttonholes are sewn on the top back piece. Find the centre and place the first buttonhole there, about 1.0 to 1.5 cm in from the folded edge. Make the buttonhole 0.6 cm longer than the diameter of the button. Make two more buttonholes, each 10 cm from the centre buttonhole. Sew on the buttons.

5 Put in the cushion insert.

APPLIQUÉ

The term 'appliqué' comes from the French 'appliquer' meaning to put on or lay on.

Appliqué has been used since ancient times, for decorative and practical purposes. An appliquéd ceremonial canopy worked in gazelle hide dating from c. 980 BC is held by an Egyptian museum.

Appliqué was probably first used to repair worn or holed fabrics by covering the damaged area with patches. In medieval Europe appliqué was used to decorate furnishings such as curtains and bed hangings, and to attach heraldic emblems and symbolic motifs to military and church garments.

Appliquéd cats for the kitchen

Perfect for a country-style kitchen, this teatowel and potholder are decorated with a fine cat figure. They are made with simple sewing and appliqué techniques, and the design would be equally suitable for a kitchen apron.

Finished sizes Teatowel 65 × 45 cm; potholder 24 × 24 cm

Materials

70 cm piece of fabric with large checks
30 cm piece of fabric with smaller checks
10 cm Vlisofix (paper coated with adhesive)
10 cm freezer paper (available from patchwork shops)
24 × 24 cm wadding
DMC stranded embroidery cotton in cream (712)
Quilting needle size 10 or small sharp sewing needle
Water-soluble pen
Pencil
Matching fabric threads

TEATOWEL
Cutting out

1 Wash and iron all fabrics before you begin to cut out.
2 From fabric with large checks cut a piece 50 × 70 cm (this piece will be used for the actual teatowel). Cut another strip of this fabric on the bias at least 50 cm long and 8 cm wide.
3 From the fabric with smaller checks cut one strip of bias at least 50 cm long and 5 cm wide. Cut another piece of this fabric on the bias 10 cm wide; the cat shapes for both the teatowel and the potholder will be cut from this piece.
4 Cut a piece of Vlisofix to fit the 10 cm wide strip.

Appliqué cats

1 With the pencil trace the two different cat shapes on page 81 onto the rough side of the freezer paper, with no seam allowance. Cut them out.
2 Iron the Vlisofix to the wrong side of the 10 cm wide strip of fabric with smaller checks.
3 Iron the cat shapes to the right side of this fabric and cut them out.
4 Remove both the Vlisofix and the freezer paper.
5 Set the shapes to one side.

To assemble

1 Hem on three sides, leaving the bottom edge raw.
2 Position the cat shapes, adhesive side down, 5 cm from the bottom edge and 7.5 cm from the side edges of the teatowel. The centre cats should be 2 cm apart. Press them in place with a hot, dry iron.
3 With one strand of cream cotton in the needle, buttonhole stitch around each cat shape. When turning corners, for example around the cat's ear, pivot the needle for three stitches to make a neat edge.
4 To make the lines for the tail, cut out one tail shape from the freezer-paper drawing and place it in position on the embroidered cat. Draw around this shape with the water-soluble pen. Turn the tail shape over and repeat for the cat facing the opposite direction.
5 With the water-soluble pen mark the neck and leg lines freehand. Stem stitch the lines with two strands of cream cotton.
6 When this stage of preparation has been completed, dab the pen marks with a damp cloth to remove them. Depending on the fabric this may need to be done several times before the marks disappear.

To prepare the bias strips

1 Take one 5 cm wide bias strip of the fabric with smaller checks. Fold in the short edges to fit the width of the teatowel and then fold the bias in half lengthwise, placing the raw edges together. Iron the bias and then

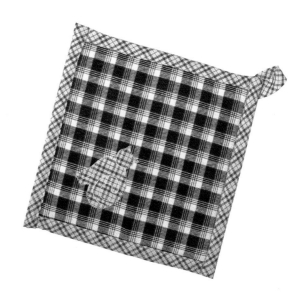

This potholder is perfect both for day-to-day use and for decoration in a country-style kitchen. Co-ordinating checks give it character.

Cat motifs

attach it to the prepared teatowel, by stitching along the bottom edge.

2 Take the 8 cm wide bias strip of the fabric with large checks, fold in the short edges to fit the width of the teatowel and then fold the bias in half lengthwise, with a 1 cm hem. Slip stitch the short edges. Place it on the teatowel so that it encases the bottom edge, and ensure that 1 cm of the bias with smaller checks is showing. Pin and tack the bias strip in place, and then top stitch across the teatowel.

POTHOLDER
Cutting out

1 Cut out two 24 x 24 cm pieces from the fabric with large checks.

2 Cut one piece of wadding the same size.

3 Cut out five pieces of 5 cm wide bias from the fabric with smaller checks.

4 With a pencil, trace one cat shape onto the rough side of the freezer paper and cut it out, with no seam allowance. Iron the shape onto the right side of the 10 cm wide Vlisofix-backed bias strip (previously prepared in the making of the teatowel), and cut it out.

5 Peel off the freezer paper and Vlisofix paper, then place the cat shape about 4 cm from the sides and 9 cm from the corner of one of the 24 x 24 cm pieces of fabric with large checks. Iron the cat shape in place as you did for the teatowel.

6 Embroider the appliquéd cat in the same way as you did for the teatowel.

To assemble

1 Place wadding between the two 24 x 24 cm pieces of fabric, which are positioned with right sides facing out.

2 Stitch around the edges with the sewing machine.

3 Trim the raw edges.

To prepare the bias strips

1 Take one of the 5 cm wide bias strips, fold and iron it in half lengthwise and hem the long sides in 1 cm. The bias strip should be 1.5 cm wide. Repeat this for a second strip.

2 Take the two strips of bias and enclose the potholder on opposite sides.

3 Pin and tack the strips in place. Repeat this procedure with the two remaining sides, enclosing the ends of the first two bias strips. Turn in the raw edges and slip stitch.

To attach the loop

1 Before top stitching, make a loop for the potholder using the last bias strip.

2 Prepare the strip as before, but machine stitch down the long side. Cut the strip to a length of 16 cm.

3 Fold the strip in half and place it at the back of the potholder with the loop facing the centre and the raw edges pointing outwards. Tack the loop in place.

4 Top stitch the four sides of the potholder including the loop. This will enclose the raw edges.

5 When the top stitching is completed, turn the loop out and spread it slightly before slip stitching the sides of the loop to hold them in place.

The decorative cat appliqués on the teatowel and potholder are attached with a bonding medium, then outlined and detailed with hand embroidery.

Pet portrait in cross stitch

The alert little cat in this life-size picture seems to reach out of the frame—perhaps in response to its owner, or some other interesting sight or sound. It is worked almost entirely in cross stitch with details added in long stitch, and the stranded cotton colours were selected for the natural impression they give.

Finished size Embroidered area 20 × 20 cm; framed area 39.5 × 40.5 cm
Graph On fold-out sheet D

Stitch
Cross stitch
Long stitch (also called straight stitch)

Materials
27 × 27 piece of 14-count Aida cloth in sky blue
DMC stranded embroidery cotton in the colours given in the key on fold-out sheet D, plus palest brown (3047) and hazelnut (898)
Tapestry needle size 26

Method
1 Following the graph and colour key on fold-out sheet D, embroider the cat design in counted cross stitch, using four strands of each appropriate coloured cotton over one square of Aida cloth.
2 When you have completed the cross stitch, embroider the whiskers in long stitch, using one strand of palest

Paint a picture with needle and thread rather than a brush and palette.

brown (3047). Embroider the paws in long stitch using two strands of hazelnut (898).
3 Mount and frame as desired.

CROSS STITCH

Cross stitch has long been used in embroidery in Europe, among both the peasantry and the ruling elite, and in fact spectacular examples of cross-stitched church embroidery dating from the fourteenth century still exist. Early cross-stitch pieces originating from Iran and India have also been identified.

Cross stitch can be worked on any fabric but is usually worked on canvas, linen or other evenwork fabric on which the strands of the weave can be counted. It is also often worked on gingham, as the squares on this style of fabric form a natural grid.

It is one of the stitches most often used in needlepoint embroidery on canvas or linen. This sort of embroidery is

often referred to as 'tapestry', because it originally imitated woven tapestries.

Cross stitch can be worked in a design that contrasts with the unworked background, or it can be worked to completely cover the base cloth, thereby giving added strength to the fabric. In Assissi embroidery the design areas are left unworked and the background is filled with cross stitches. Threads made of cotton, linen, wool or silk are used.

In its simplest form cross stitch is worked from left to right and back again, with the first 'run' creating a row of diagonal or half cross stitches and the second run completing the crosses.

This charming framed picture would make a treasured gift for a cat-loving friend or family member, and you could adapt the colours to imitate the coat of a favourite pet.

French knot brooch for a cat lover

Create your own piece of heirloom jewellery by embroidering this nostalgic motif, featuring an exquisite French-knot tabby cat peeking out from a floral bower. A particularly effective result is achieved by using a large variety of colours and stitches within a small area.

Finished size Motif 4 x 3 cm

Stitches
French knot
Detached chain stitch
Satin stitch

Materials
Small piece of pale blue finely woven cotton or linen
Crewel embroidery needle size 10
Small quantities of DMC stranded embroidery cotton in white, steel grey (317), pale steel grey (318), dove grey (415), light rose pink (894), medium rose pink (776), dark rose pink (891), light tangerine (742), light pistachio green (368) and one strand each of blue (813) and black (310)
Small piece of wadding
Brooch frame
Thin piece of white card
Tracing paper
Pencil
Adhesive

Embroidery
1 First buy a brooch frame so that you will know the required finished size before you begin embroidering the motif. Draw around the plastic 'protector' from the brooch frame to make an outline on the fabric which will act as a guide for the size of the embroidered insert. With tracing paper and a pencil copy the outline of the

Embroidery motif

French knots, detached chain stitch and satin stitch create a vibrant, densely planted garden, a perfect background for a cat.

cat as well as a suggestion of the flower shapes and then trace them onto the fabric.
2 Use one strand of thread and one twist for the closely packed French knots on the cat and flower centres, and one strand for flowers and leaves.
3 To form the eyes of the cat first work tiny horizontal satin stitches in blue, outline them with tiny horizontal back stitches in black (310), and make a vertical stitch for the pupils. Define the nose and mouth in light rose pink (894). After finishing the body, split one strand of white thread and with a half-strand work a few whiskers.
4 Embroider the flowers close together using detached chain stitch and French knots. Sew leaves among the flowers and fill any gaps with the cat colours.
5 Iron the wrong side of the fabric using a damp cloth to protect the embroidered area.

To assemble
1 Use the brooch protector again to draw an outline on a thin piece of white card. Cut out the oval shape, then trim it to fit just inside the rim of the plastic protector.
2 Cut the fabric around the embroidery leaving enough to run a gathering stitch around it close to the edge.
3 Place a small piece of wadding, cut to the appropriate size, on the wrong side of the embroidery, then place the card on the wadding and pull the gathering stitches firmly. Check that the design is centrally placed and, before ending off the thread, check that the embroidery fits snugly into the cavity of the plastic protector.
4 With a dab of adhesive attach the embroidery to the bed of the brooch and press the frame down.

The finished embroidery can be worn as a brooch, or hung on a chain as a pendant. Either way, you'll have an ornament to be proud of.

Mother cat and kittens

This pretty cat protectively wrapping her tail around her kittens would be a quaint decoration for any room of the house, not just a child's bedroom. The mother cat has a firm base to ensure that she will sit securely wherever you perch her and her family.

Finished sizes Mother cat 25 × 16 cm; kittens 9 × 5 cm
Patterns On fold-out sheet F

Stitches

Satin stitch
Stem stitch

Materials

60 cm of cotton fabric for cat
Small amount of contrasting fabric for kittens
Washable soft toy filling
Embroidery threads for cats' faces
Two buttons for mother cat's eyes (optional)
Ribbon for bows
Firm plastic for base
Tracing paper and pencil

Mother cat

1 Using tracing paper and a pencil copy the pattern pieces on fold-out sheet F, adding 1 cm seams all around. Mark the eyes, nose and mouth on the piece for the front. Trace the shapes onto the wrong side of the fabric and cut out back and front pieces and the tail, all with a 1 cm seam allowance. On the right side of the front piece mark the positions of eyes, nose and mouth.
2 Embroider the face, using satin stitch for the nose, stem stitch for the mouth and straight stitch for whiskers. Use buttons for the eyes or embroider them in satin stitch.
3 Stitch the body pieces together, leaving an opening at the bottom.
4 Clip around the seams for ease on the curves. Turn the fabric to the right side and stuff the body with filling.
5 For the base cut an 8.5 cm diameter circle from a piece of firm plastic (an icecream container is ideal) then cut a slightly larger circle of material, allowing enough to turn under the clipping edges. Sew the base to the cat.
6 Stuff and attach the tail, then tie ribbons around the cat's neck.

Kittens (make two)

1 Trace the kitten pattern onto two pieces of contrasting fabric following the procedure as for the cat.

2 Embroider the kittens' faces in stem stitch.
3 Stitch the pieces together, leaving an opening at the bottom. Turn to the right side, stuff the bodies and then close the opening.
4 Position the kittens so that the mother cat's tail wraps around them, and slip stitch the kittens to the cat's base. Catch the end of the cat's tail to her body. Tie ribbon bows to the kittens.

Attaching kittens to the base of mother cat

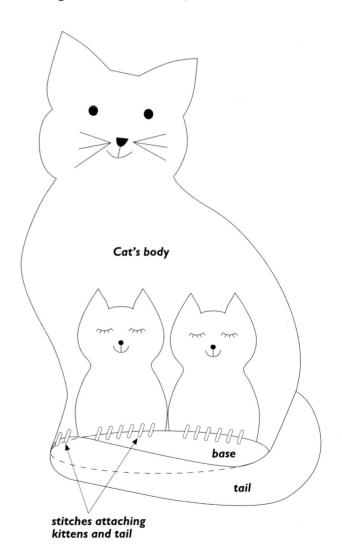

Cat's body

base

tail

*stitches attaching
kittens and tail*

The kittens nestle snugly against their alert mother, held firmly in place by rows of stitches.

Bookmark with cross-stitched cats

This whimsical bookmark is decorated with a cute collection of cross-stitched cats who come not only in a variety of poses and colours but also with sound effects. The piece is beautifully finished with floral cross-stitched details and a small tassel.

Finished size 22 × 5 cm, not including tassel

Stitches
Cross stitch
French knot

Materials
23 cm of 5 cm wide white 14-count Aida cloth band
23 cm lightweight iron-on interfacing
DMC stranded embroidery cotton in the colours given
  in the key
White tassel

Method
1 Embroider the cats and the borders as indicated on the graph and colour key. Work in counted cross stitch, using two strands of embroidery cotton over one square of Aida cloth.
2 When you have completed the embroidery iron the interfacing on the wrong side. Make a 1 cm hem at the top and fold the bottom in to make a point. Catch the hem and folded point on the wrong side.
3 Attach the tassel.

DMC colour key

╱	414	*Medium dark grey*
╎	415	*Dove grey*
○		*White*
╲	739	*Beige*
╲	922	*Dark orange*
■	310	*Black*
✕	368	*Light pistachio green*
○	893	*Sugar pink*
•	310	*Black French knot for eyes and nose*

Outlines:
Top cat use 414 (medium dark grey) for outline and 310 (black) for whiskers.
Centre cat use 922 (dark orange) for outline and 310 (black) for whiskers.
Bottom cat use 310 (black) for outline.

Embroidery motifs

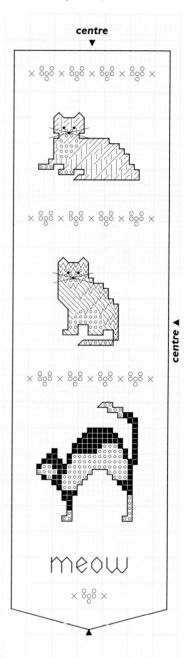

Next time you have to put down a good book to attend to the demands of your cat, mark your place with this charming bookmark.

A kitten for baby

This adorable soft and colourful kitten with a cheeky smile is just the right size for tiny hands to grasp. Its simple and sturdy design means it will come through the most enthusiastic play sessions unscathed; but be sure to make it from materials that can stand up to repeated washing.

Finished size 13 × 12 cm
Pattern On fold-out sheet C

Stitches

Buttonhole stitch
Detached chain stitch
Padded satin stitch
Pistil stitch
Satin stitch
Stem stitch

Materials

Small scrap of striped or floral material
Scrap of plain-coloured material
Small amount of washable toy filling
Ribbon for neck bow
DMC stranded embroidery cotton in dark blue-green (501), brown-green (844), dark dusty pink (223) and dark mauve (3041) (or your choice of colours)
Greaseproof paper
HB pencil

Body

1 With the pencil trace the body pieces on fold-out sheet C onto greaseproof paper, and add 0.7 cm all around for seam allowance.
2 Using the greaseproof paper pattern, cut out two body sections in striped material.
3 With the right sides together, machine stitch a 0.7 cm seam allowance. Leave the body open between the points marked A and B on the cutting pattern. Clip the seam allowance.
4 Turn the fabric through to the right side. Firmly stuff the body with fibre filling and stitch the opening closed.

Head

1 Using the greaseproof pattern and an HB pencil, trace the kitten's facial features onto the plain material and work the embroidery. Use one strand of brown-green (844) to embroider the eyebrow. Work the eye colour in satin stitch using two strands of dark blue-green (501), and sew the pupil in detached chain stitch, using two

strands of dark blue-green. Embroider the whiskers in dark mauve (3041) in pistil stitch. Work the nose and mouth in two strands of dark dusty pink (223), using padded satin stitch and stem stitch.
2 Cut out two head sections (noting the grain line and correctly positioning the facial features). With the right sides together, machine stitch all around the edges taking a 0.7 cm seam allowance. Carefully slash back only where indicated on the cutting pattern. Clip the seam allowance round the curves.
3 Turn the fabric through to the right side and firmly stuff the head with fibre filling.

To assemble

1 Oversew the slit and sew the head firmly to the body by hand.
2 Tie a ribbon around the neck and secure it with a couple of small invisible stitches.
3 Work a small buttonholed bar from the end of the tail to the kitten's back so that the tail will not fit into a baby's mouth and present a choking hazard.

As a safety precaution the kitten's long curly tail is securely stitched to its back, so that it cannot fit into baby's mouth.

Cheerful fabric and brightly coloured embroidery thread make a toy that will delight any young child. The ribbon adds a cheeky finishing touch.

Stitch library

Back stitch

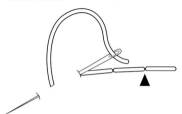

Bullion stitch

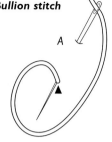 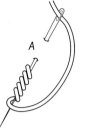 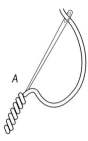

1 Pick up fabric the size of the knot

2 Twist thread around needle

3 Pull needle through and insert again at A

Buttonhole stitch

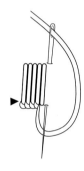

Chain stitch

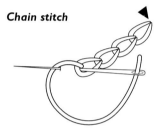

Colonial knot

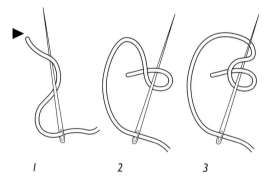

1   2   3   4   5

Cross stitch

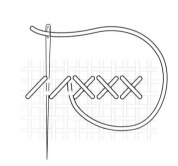

Detached chain stitch

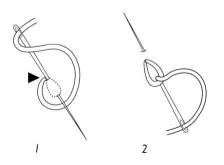

1   2

Eyelet stitch

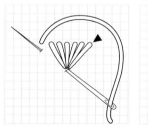

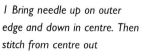

1 Bring needle up on outer edge and down in centre. Then stitch from centre out

2 Complete eyelet to form square with an even number of stitches across each side

French knot

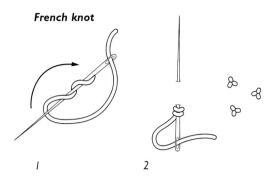

1   2

Half cross stitch

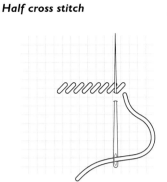

Herringbone stitch

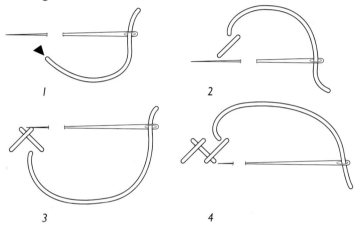

1   2

3   4

Ladder stitch

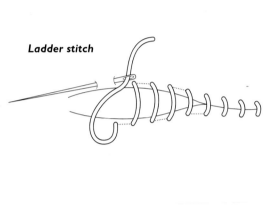

Padded buttonhole stitch

1 Fill in area with chain stitch

2 Work eyelet over area. Bring needle up on outer edge and down in centre. Then stitch from centre out

Padded satin stitch

1 Outline area with split stitch

2 Fill in with chain stitch

3 Cover area with satin stitch

Pistil stitch

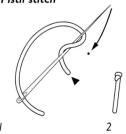

1   2

Running stitch

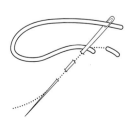

Satin stitch

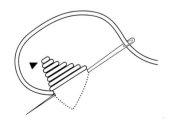

Split stitch

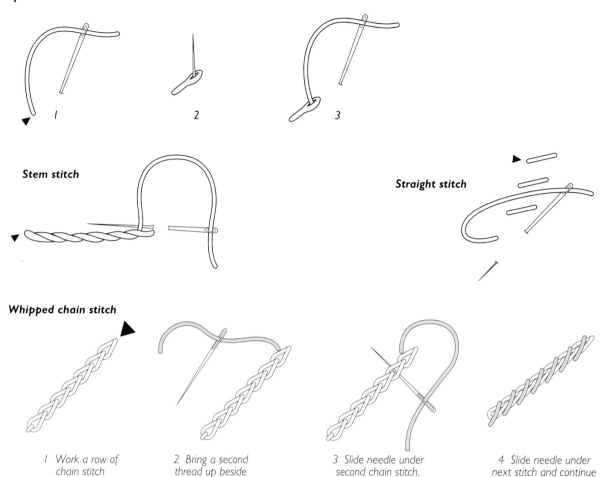

Stem stitch

Straight stitch

Whipped chain stitch

1 Work a row of chain stitch

2 Bring a second thread up beside first chain stitch

3 Slide needle under second chain stitch. Do not pierce fabric

4 Slide needle under next stitch and continue until completed

Knitting stitch embroidery

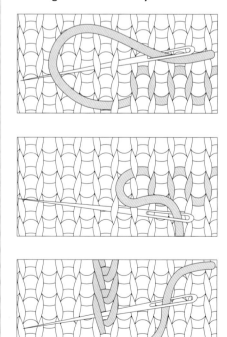

Knitting abbreviations

alt=alternate; beg=begin/ning; cont=continue; dec=decrease, decreasing; foll=follows, following; garter st=every row knit; inc=increase, increasing; incl=inclusive, including; K=knit; 0=(zero) no sts, rows or times; P=purl; patt=pattern; psso=pass slipped stitch over; purl fabric (reverse stocking st)=1 row purl (right side), 1 row knit (wrong side); rem=remaining; sl=slip; st/s=stitch/es; stocking st=1 row knit, 1 row purl; tbl=through back of loop; tog=together; ybk=yarn back—take yarn under needle from purling position into knitting position, without making a st; yft=yarn front—bring yarn under needle from knitting position into purling position, without making a st; yfwd=yarn forward—bring yarn under needle, then over into a knitting position again, thus making a st; yrn=yarn round needle—take yarn right around needle into purling position, thus making a stitch

Index

Published by Murdoch Books®, a division of Murdoch Magazines Pty Ltd,
45 Jones Street, Ultimo NSW 2007

Managing Editor, Craft & Gardening: Christine Eslick
Editor: Diana Hill
Designer: Michèle Lichtenberger
Photographer: Andre Martin
Stylist: Georgina Dolling
Illustrator: Stephen Pollitt

Projects designed and made by Bonnie Arthurson (pp. 11, 26, 30, 68, 84); John Bowler (p. 16);
Greg Cheetham (p. 44); Robyn Cooper (p. 20); Ludmila Hayes (p. 82); Jenny Jansen (pp. 33, 50, 70, 90);
Kristen McCallum (pp. 36, 74); Maria Ragan (pp. 6, 38, 56); Ragnhild Rees (pp. 23, 28, 47, 54, 62, 76, 79);
Sabina Robba (p. 64); Stella Robinson (pp. 14, 52, 60, 66, 86, 88); Jo Williams (p. 41)

CEO & Publisher: Anne Wilson
International Sales Director: Mark Newman

National Library of Australia
Cataloguing-in-Publication Data
Cat Craft Collection. Includes index. ISBN 0 86411 718 3
1. Handicrafts. I. Title: Better Homes and Gardens (North Sydney, N.S.W). 746

Printed by Prestige Litho, Queensland
First published 1998

Acknowledgements
The publisher would like to acknowledge the following for assistance with photography: Home & Garden; Dulux
Paints; The Australian Museum; Petsworld, Leichhardt; The Cat Protection Society; Doff's Kitchen; Porters Paints

Every effort has been made to ensure the availability of materials used in this book, but the
availability of particular materials, colours and fabrics cannot be guaranteed.